~ SPITFIRE ~

A LOOK BACK OVER THE GATE

A PICTORIAL TRIBUTE TO BRITISH GATE GUARDS

by

RAY C. COULSON

This book is dedicated to my wife Melanie
for her help and tolerance with my passion for
the Spitfire over the last seven years.

Publisher: R. C. Coulson, 81 Southbank Road, Coventry CV6 1FB West Midlands.
ISBN 0 9523825 0 4
Printed by I.P.H. Litho (Coventry) Limited, Unit D3, Wolston Business Park, Coventry CV8 3FU - August 1994

No part of this publication may be reproduced by any means whatsoever without the written permission of the publisher.

Introduction

The story of the Spitfire Guards began in the late 1940's when it became the trend for R.A.F. Stations, mostly with Battle of Britain connections, to display a Spitfire. By 1960 a mere 43 remained, standing guard at R.A.F. and A.T.C. establishments, but as the years passed, one or two ended up on fire dumps and were sold by tender, others were donated to museums and some went abroad. In the mid-1980's three were exchanged for aeroplanes required by the R.A.F. Museum and by early 1988 the number had fallen to seventeen.

With the exception of two Spitfires, TB752 at R.A.F. Manston, and LA255, at R.A.F. Wittering, November 1989 saw the removal of the last Spitfire Gate Guard. This was PM651, which had been displayed at R.A.F. Benson for 16 years. A tradition which blossomed in the early 1950's and continued for nearly 40 years, had come to an end.

In April 1987, the M.O.D. set up a Working Party on Historic Aircraft to advise on the policy aspects of retention, maintenance and deployment of non-flying historic R.A.F. aircraft. The policy of withdrawing Spitfire Gate Guardians stemmed from a recommendation of the Working Party, whose members were concerned by the poor state of preservation of many of the aircraft and were anxious to prevent further deterioration of such valuable assets. In February 1988 the decision was taken by the Air Force Board to replace these aircraft with glass-fibre replicas. I felt that this was a chapter in the history of the Spitfire which should not go unrecorded and this book is a pictorial tribute to these aeroplanes. As their detailed histories have been covered by other authors, I have chosen to simply include abbreviated histories as an introduction to each set of captioned pictures which span up to five decades. These Spitfires are seen as they were, some whilst still flying, all while on display, some showing obvious neglect and the ravages of our inclement weather, and others during restoration - a credit to those who have worked on them. Each history concludes with a look beyond the gate to see what has become of them since being relieved of guard duty.

This book is solely devoted to Spitfires which, at some time or other, were on Gate Guard duty with the R.A.F., including four at overseas stations. Other Air Forces around the world flew Spitfires and some were eventually displayed. Perhaps a book on these overseas Guards may be considered in the future and the author would welcome any photographic contributions to this end. Neither does this book cover those British Spitfire Guards which, over the years were scrapped after suffering neglect and irreparable damage. Although I am aware of their service, I have chosen to exclude them from this compilation. This book is dedicated to those still in existence and I hope the reader will be able to use this work as a reference to locate and visit some of them.

The flying career of SL574 ended on the 20th of September 1959. Following engine problems, her pilot, Air Vice Marshall H. J. Maguire made a forced landing on a cricket pitch at Bromley, Kent. A fire engine is in attendance, as a crew from Martlesham Heath begin the task of dismantling SL574 for her journey home by road. *(Ron W. Cranham)*

Acknowledgements

In compiling this book I have received help from many people, and I would like to express my thanks. Firstly to Ken Woolley, who 25 years ago, gave a lot of encouragement to a boy, fresh out of school, who was developing a fascination for the Spitfire.

In more recent times to Ron Cranham, who has allowed me to chose freely from his extensive collection of photographs. Were it not for his constant help and support this book would have not been possible. It therefore filled me with great sadness to hear of his sudden death before he had the opportunity to see the book to which he had contributed so much. I always found Ron a friendly and charming man, who will be missed by everyone who had the privilege of knowing him.

A special thank you to Spitfire Historian, Peter R. Arnold, who always found the time to answer my many queries concerning detail points about some of the Guards. Peter also helped me complete the work by filling gaps in this compilation when other sources proved fruitless. To Stanley R. Bates who was instrumental in seeing the collection of photographs I had amassed over the years, become the book you have before you.

I must mention the R.A.F. Stations and their Public Relations Officers, Spitfire owners, museums, fellow collectors, and everyone else who has supported me, offered advice and photographs over the last seven years.

To Mr. J.S. Cox of the A.H.B., who supplied details of the decision to withdraw Spitfires from station gates, and to Mike and Christine Jennings-Bates, the printers, who gave unstinting support and encouragement with this book.

In conclusion, a list of those who have given help:

P.R. Arnold, Spitfire Historian
Air Cadet
Aviation Photo News
S.R. Bates
J. Bishop Flt. Lt. R.A.F. Volunteer Reserve.
G. Bowtle
P.J. Burgess Sgt.
S.J. Chamberlain Sqn.Ldr., B.Eng.
P. Charles
A. Chivers
R.W. Cranham
P. Crouch Cpl.
Crown Copyright/MOD. Reproduced with the permission of the controller of the HMSO.
City of Stoke-on-Trent Museum & Art Gallery
E.K. Coventry
J.S. Cox, B.A., M.A.
Daily Express
R. Deacon
L.E. Deal
C. Denny
J.M. Dibbs
C. Du Vé
I.S. Duncan
T. Fairclough
R.S. Fell
D.H. Fife Sqn. Ldr., R.A.F. Volunteer Reserve
C.J. Foulds
B. Griffiths
F.K. Griffiths
R.Griffiths Flt.Lt. R.A.F. Volunteer Reserve
D.J. Green Gp.Capt. (retired)
P.T.H. Green (Historian)
C. Harness Sgt.
A.M. Hewitt
Historic Flying Limited
M. and C. Jennings-Bates
I. King
N.A.MacDougall
T. Maddock
R.J. Major Sqn.Ldr. (retired)
Military Aviation Photographs
Musee De L'Air et de L'Espace (France)
Museum of Flight (Scotland)
Muzeum Lotnictwa Astronautyki (Poland)
National Aviation Museum (Canada)
P. Owen
R. Paver
A. Pearcy
Personal Plane Services
R.A.F. Abingdon
R.A.F. Bentley Priory
R.A.F. Halton
R.A.F. Leuchars
R.A.F. Manston
R.A.F. Museum, Hendon
R.A.F. News
R.A.F. Shawbury
R.A.F. St. Athan
R.A.F. Turnhouse
R.A.F. Wittering
N. Randell
G. Riley
N. Riordan
C.L. Rispler
R.N.Z.A.F. Museum, Wigram (New Zealand)
W. Rouse
T. Routsis
C.A. Rousell
C. Shelton
P. Shelley
J.G. Shutte
The Museum of Science and Industry in Manchester
The Spitfire Society
B. Tallon (Photographer) Western Canada Aviation Museum
A.S. Thomas
G.P. Trant (Historian)
Ulster Aviation Society (Northern Ireland)
A. Watson
R. Weston

List of Abbreviations

'A' type roundel, under wing, red, white and blue, 50 inches diameter.
A.F.S. Advanced Flying School.
A.F.D.S. Air Fighter Development Squadron.
A.G.T. Airwork General Trading.
A.H.B. Air Historical Branch.
A.O.C. Air Officer Commanding.
A.P.N. Aviation Photo News.
A.T.C. Air Training Corps.
'B' Wing armament: one 20 mm cannon and two .303 machine guns per wing.
B.B.M.F. Battle of Britain Memorial Flight.
'C' or Universal Wing armament: two .303 machine guns and one 20 mm cannon, or two 20 mm cannons, per wing.
'C' type roundel, under wing, red, white and blue, 32 inches diameter.
C.A.A.C.U. Civil Anti-Aircraft Co-operation Unit.
C.F.E. Central Fighter Establishment.
C.G.S. Central Gunnery School.
'E' wing armament: one .5 machine gun and one 20 mm cannon per wing.
E.C.F.S. Empire Central Flying School.
F Fighter role.
F.C.C. & R.S. Fighter Command Control and Reporting School.
F.P.T. Ferry Pilot Training.
F.R. Fighter Reconnaissance.
F.R.S. Flying Refresher School.
F.T.U. Ferry Training School.
H.F.L. Historic Flying Limited.
L.F. Low Altitude Fighter role.
M.A.P. Military Aviation Photographs.
M Suffix for instructional airframe number.
Met. Meteorological.
M.O.D. Ministry of Defence.
M.U. Maintenance Unit.
O.C.U. Operational Conversion Unit.
O.F.M.C. Old Flying Machine Company.
O.T.U. Operational Training Unit.
P.R. Photographic Reconnaissance.
P.R.U. Photographic Reconnaissance Unit.
R.A.F.M. Royal Air Force Museum.
R.Aux.A.F. Royal Auxillary Air Force.
R.C.A.F. Royal Canadian Air Force.
R. Neth.A.F. Royal Netherlands Air Force.
R.N.Z.A.F. Royal New Zealand Air Force.
R.N.Z.A.F.M. Royal New Zealand Air Force Museum.
S.T.T. School of Technical Training.
T.A.F. Tactical Air Force.
THUM Temperature and Humidity Flight.
W.B. of G.B. War Birds of Great Britain.

Contents

	Serial	Mark	Present Location	Page
◆	AR614	F.VC	H.F.L. Audley End, Saffron Walden, Essex, U.K. (Owned by Sir Tim Wallis, The Alpine Fighter Collection, New Zealand).	1
†	BL614	F.VB	The Museum of Science and Industry in Manchester, Lancs., U.K.	3
◆*	BM597	F.VB	H.F.L., Audley End, Saffron Walden, Essex, U.K. (Owned by Guy Black, Historic Aircraft Collection)	5
◆†	EP120	L.F.VB	H.F.L., Audley End, Saffron Walden, Essex, U.K. (Owned by Stephen Grey, The Fighter Collection)	7
◆†	MK356	L.F.IXC	R.A.F. St. Athan, Glamorgan, Wales. (Under restoration for BBMF).	9
‡	MK732	L.F.IXC	R.Neth.A.F., Deelen or Glize Rijen Air Bases, Netherlands.	11
	MK959	L.F.IXC	R.Neth.A.F., Deelen Air Base, Netherlands.	13
	MT847	F.R.XIVE	R.A.F. Aerospace Museum, Cosford, Salop, U.K.	15
	RM694	F.XIVC	Florida U.S.A.	17
	RR263	L.F.XVIE	Musée de L'Air et de L'Espace, Le Bourget, France.	19
†‡*	RW382	L.F.XVIE	H.F.L., Audley End, Saffron Walden, Essex, U.K. (Owned by David C. Tallichet)	21
◆	RW386	L.F.XVIE	Florida, U.S.A. (Stored)	23
	RW388	L.F.XVIE	Stoke-on-Trent City Museum & Art Gallery, Staffs., U.K.	25
	RW393	L.F.XVIE	R.A.F. St. Athan, Glamorgan, Wales. (Stored).	27
◆	SL542	L.F.XVIE	Lakeland, Florida, U.S.A. (Owned by Mike Araldi).	29
†•	SL574	L.F.XVIE	San Diego Aerospace Museum, California, U.S.A.	31
	SL674	L.F.XVIE	R.A.F. St. Athan, Glamorgan, Wales. (Stored).	33
†	SM411	L.F.XVIE	Muzeum Lotnictwa Astronautyki, Krakow, Poland.	35
◆*	TB252	L.F.XVIE	H.F.L., Audley End, Saffron Walden, Essex, U.K. (Owned by Nicholas Springer)	37
†	TB382	L.F.XVIE	R.A.F. Exhibition Flight, R.A.F. Abingdon, Oxon, U.K.	39
	TB752	L.F.XVIE	R.A.F. Manston, Kent, U.K.	41
◆	TD135	L.F.XVIE	Genesio State, New York, U.S.A.	43
‡*	TD248	L.F.XVIE	B.A.C. Aviation, Earls Colne, Essex, U.K. (Owned by Eddie K. Coventry)	45
‡	TE184	L.F.XVIE	Myrick Aviation, Jersey, Channel Isles.	47
	TE214	L.F.XVIE	Western Canada Aviation Museum, Winnipeg, Canada.	49
•	TE288	L.F.XVIE	R.N.Z.A.F. Museum, R.N.Z.A.F. Wigram, Christchurch, New Zealand.	51
†	TE311	L.F.XVIE	R.A.F. Exhibition Flight, R.A.F. Abingdon, Oxon, U.K.	53
†‡	TE356	Ł.F.XVIE	Evergreen Ventures, Pinal Air Park, Marana, Arizona, U.S.A. (Owned by Delford M. Smith)	55
†‡	TE384	L.F.XVIE	Toowoomba, Queensland, Australia. (Owned by Hockey Treloar Syndicate)	57
	TE392	L.F.XVIE	Florida, U.S.A. (Stored).	59
	TE462	L.F.XVIE	Museum of Flight, East Fortune, Lothian, Scotland.	61
◆†*	TE476	L.F.XVIE	Personal Plane Services, Wycombe Air Park, Bucks., U.K. (Owned by Kermit Weeks)	63
†	PM651	P.R.XIX	R.A.F. St. Athan, Glamorgan, Wales (Stored).	65
†‡	PS853	P.R.XIX	B.B.M.F., R.A.F. Coningsby, Lincs., U.K.	67
†‡	PS915	P.R.XIX	B.B.M.F., R.A.F. Coningsby, Lincs., U.K.	69
†	LA198	F.21	R.A.F. St. Athan, Glamorgan, Wales. (Stored).	71
	LA226	F.21	R.A.F. St. Athan, Glamorgan, Wales, (Stored)	73
	LA255	F.21	R.A.F. Wittering, Cambs., U.K.	75
	PK624	F.22	R.A.F. St. Athan, Glamorgan, Wales (Stored)	77
	PK664	F.22	R.A.F. St. Athan, Glamorgan, Wales (Stored)	79
	PK683	F.24	Hall of Aviation, Southampton, Hampshire, U.K.	81
	PK724	F.24	R.A.F. Museum, Hendon, London, U.K.	83
	VN485	F.24	Imperial War Museum, Duxford, Cambs., U.K	85

* A deal between Historic Flying Limited and the R.A.F. amounted to an exchange. The R.A.F. received, for display at the R.A.F. Museum, Hendon, a Curtiss D40-N and a Bristol Beaufort. They also received 12 glass-fibre Spitfire and Hurricane replicas, for display at chosen R.A.F. Stations. In return, H.F.L. received five real Spitfires.
• Participated in the film "Reach for the Sky".
† Participated in the film "The Battle of Britain". } For further details see page 87
‡ Restored to flying condition.
◆ Under Restoration.

List of Sources

Spitfire - The Story of a Famous Fighter.
Bruce Robertson (Harleyford Publications).

Spitfire The History.
Eric B. Morgan and Edward Shacklady (Key Publications).

Spitfire Survivors Round the World.
Gordon Riley and Graham Trant (Aston Publications).

The Spitfire V Manual.
R.A.F. Museum, Hendon (Arms and Armour Press).

The Spitfire Story.
Dr. Alfred Price (Janes).

Veteran and Vintage Aircraft.
Leslie Hunt (Published by L. Hunt).

Wrecks and Relics 8th Edition.
Ken Ellis (Merseyside Aviation Society Publication).

"Born Again" Spitfire PS915.
Wally Rouse (Midland Counties Publications (Aerophile) Limited).

AR614

Spitfire F.VC AR614 was taken on charge by the R.A.F. in August 1942. The following month saw her issued to No.312 (Czech) Squadron. In May 1943 she was damaged in action and after repair was stored, joining No.610 (County of Chester) Squadron in November 1943. She flew with this unit until January 1944. After a very brief spell with No. 130 (Punjab) Squadron, AR614 transferred to No.222 (Natal) Squadron, operating with them until May. Her final flying unit was No.53 O.T.U. with whom she flew from September 1944 until June 1945. The following month AR614 was issued to St. Athan as an insructional airframe. By 1949 she could be seen on display at Padgate, moving to West Kirby during the 1950's. By 1958 she had transferred to Hednesford but before the year was out she was issued to Bridgnorth. This proved to be her last posting, as in 1963 AR614 found herself on the dump at Dishforth. She was sold the following year, and travelled to Canada. After spending several years in storage this Spitfire was sold, and at last her restoration began. During 1992 AR614 was purchased by the Duxford based O.F.M.C. and her rebuild continued. In August 1994 she was acquired by Sir Tim Wallace for the Alpine Fighter Collection, New Zealand, and is being restored by H.F.L. Audley End.

Spitfire F.VC AR614 circa 1957, whilst displayed at West Kirby, painted in the all silver finish common for the period. This aeroplane was damaged four times during W.W. II, on one occasion she was hit by flak but thankfully made it back home. *(Ron W. Cranham)*

In 1958 AR614 was transferred to Bridgnorth on the back of a "Queen Mary" transporter. The incorrect 'M' number was applied to the fuselage at some time, and as her original documentation had been lost it was some years before her true identity was rediscovered.
(John Shutte)

On her wheels at last, repainted and sporting a red spinner. This proved to be the last posting for AR614.
(Ron W. Cranham)

Looking rather forlorn in 1963, languishing on the dump at Dishforth. From here she was sold by tender and travelled to Canada.
(Ron W. Cranham)

After nearly 30 years abroad, AR614 returned home to her then owners, The Old Flying Machine Company for restoration.
(Peter R. Arnold Collection)

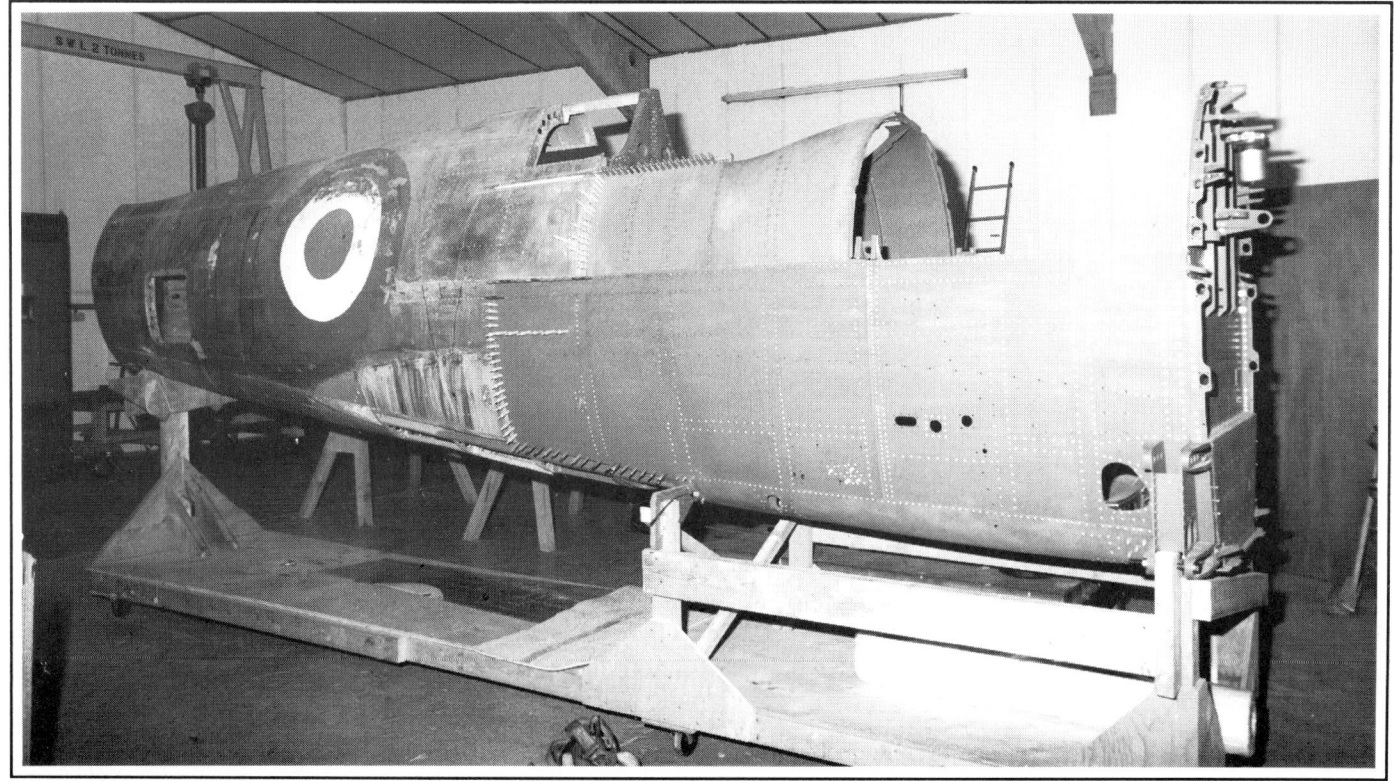

BL614

Spitfire F.VB BL614 was taken on charge by the R.A.F. in January 1942. Her first three units all flew from Drem in Scotland. Firstly she joined No. 611 (West Lancashire) Squadron, staying with them from February until March 1942. She was then transferred to No. 242. In August she moved once again to No. 222 (Natal) Squadron. March 1943 saw BL614 fly south, being issued to No. 64 Squadron to Hornchurch. Her final operational unit was No. 118 Squadron which she joined in September 1943. Two months later BL614 was transferred to No. 2 School of Technical Training at Cosford as an instructional airframe, then moving to No. 6 School of Technical Training at Hednesford in December. This Spitfire moved to Bridgnorth in April 1948 and during the 1950's was displayed at Credenhill, remaining there until 1967, when she travelled to Henlow for use in the film "The Battle of Britain". After her role in the film, she was stored at Wattisham until late 1972, then transferred to Colerne for display. Eventually BL614 joined the collection of aeroplanes displayed at St. Athan, arriving in 1975. Her final move came during 1982 when she was donated to the Greater Manchester Museum of Science and Industry, Aviation Gallery.

Spitfire F.VB BL614 seen at Credenhill in August 1961, looking somewhat neglected with various access panels and main undercarriage fairings missing.
(Ron W. Cranham)

Due to a mix-up with another Spitfire in the 1950's, BL614 was issued with the incorrect 'M' number. When restored in the early 1960's she was given the wrong identity, thus becoming 'AB871' coded SH-S.
(M.A.P.)

Pictured in June 1974 at Colerne. Whilst having her many coats of paint removed, her true identity was discovered. So 'AB871' was restored as BL614 coded ZD-F, the markings she wore whilst flying with No. 222 Squadron in support of the Dieppe raid in August 1942.

(Ron W. Cranham)

Taken in 1985, BL614 now displayed in her final home, The Aviation Gallery of the Manchester Museum of Science and Industry.

(Alan M. Hewitt)

BM597

Spitfire F.VB BM597 was taken on charge by the R.A.F. in April 1942. She was issued to No. 315 (Deblin) Squadron, her stay with this Polish unit was brief, moving to No. 317 (Wilno) Squadron during September. In February 1943, BM597 suffered a flying accident and following repair she was used for development work at Vickers-Armstrong. A long period in store followed, then in April 1945 she joined her final flying unit, No. 58 O.T.U., serving with them until October 1945. BM597 was then down-graded to an instructional airframe and transferred to No. 4 School of Technical Training at St. Athan.

During the 1950's she began her new role as display aircraft, firstly at Hednesford, then at Bridgnorth. When this station closed BM597 was issued to Church Fenton, arriving in 1964. With the making of the film "The Battle of Britain" she was removed from display and taken to Pinewood Studios where she was used to make the moulds for the replicas used in the film. BM597 returned to Church Fenton during 1969. This Spitfire was part of the R.A.F./H.F.L. exchange deal and as such was removed from display in May 1989 and is currently being restored to flying condition at their Audley End facility

Spitfire F.VB BM597, seen here in the late 1950's, displayed at R.A.F. Bridgnorth. *(Ron W. Cranham)*

In 1964, BM597 was transferred to Church Fenton, now looking more warlike in camouflage scheme, bearing the markings of a No. 609 (West Riding) Squadron aeroplane but in place of her serial number is her Maintenance Command Number - 5718M, barely visible in this shot.

(Ray C. Coulson)

BM597 in 1987, still at Church Fenton. Two years after this photograph was taken, it went to the Cambridge home of Historic Flying Limited, who took over ownership as part of the R.A.F./H.F.L. exchange deal. *(M.A.P.)*

In store at the H.F.L. hangar at Audley End in September 1992. BM597 patiently awaits her turn to be restored to flying condition. *(Ray C. Coulson)*

EP120

Spitfire L.F.VB EP120 was taken on charge by the R.A.F. in May 1942. The following month she joined No. 501 (County of Gloucester) Squadron R.Aux.A.F. serving with them until September, when she was transferred to No. 19 Squadron. Her stay here was brief, moving to her last operational unit, No. 402 (Winnipeg Bear) Squadron R.C.A.F. in April 1943. In February 1944 EP120 suffered a flying accident and, following repair, moved to No. 53 O.T.U., serving with them from October 1944 until July 1945, when she ceased flying, moving to No. 4 School of Technical Training at St. Athan. Eventually EP120 was used for display at Wilmslow and Bircham Newton before transferring to Boulmer in the early 1960's. During 1967 this Spitfire travelled to Henlow for use in the film "The Battle of Britain". After the film she was restored and in 1970 was placed on display at Wattisham until 1989 when she was placed in store at St. Athan. In 1993 EP120 joined The Fighter Collection at Duxford. In payment the R.A.F. M. received a F86 Sabre which once flew with the R.A.F. EP120 is now in the very capable hands of H.F.L. at Audley End where she is being restored to flying condition.

Spitfire L.F.VB EP120 seen at Wilmslow in Cheshire during the late 1950's. This was her first posting as a display aircraft, following her use as an instructional airframe at St. Athan in the post war years.
(Ron W. Cranham)

September 1963 and EP120 had gone on display at Boulmer. Not only had she gained a camouflage scheme but also a four bladed propeller. At that time Spitfire TD135 was on the dump at Dishforth and a good source of spares for the restoration of EP120.
(Ron W. Cranham)

Like many other Spitfires, this one appeared in the film "The Battle of Britain". After filming, EP120 was restored and finished in the markings of a No. 19 Squadron aircraft, a unit she flew with in September 1942, and placed on display at Wattisham in 1970.

(Crown Copyright/M.O.D.)

EP120 in the hangar of Historic Flying Limited at Audley End in June 1994. Soon she will be re-skinned as part of her restoration to flying condition.

(Richard H. Paver)

MK356

Spitfire L.F.IXC MK356 was taken on charge by the R.A.F. in February 1944. In March of the same year she was issued to No. 443 (Hornet) Squadron R.C.A.F. and served with them until a flying accident required her to be sent to No. 83 Group Support Unit for repairs in August 1944. MK356 may have remained in store for a considerable time as she ended her days as an instructional airframe at No. 1 School of Technical Training, Halton, arriving there in October 1945. During 1951 this Spitfire was placed on display at Hawkinge, moving to Locking in the early 1960's. She moved to Henlow during 1967 for use in the film "The Battle of Britain", following which she was placed in store. In August 1969 she was placed with the St. Athan collection. After nearly 20 years at the museum, MK356 travelled to Abingdon for assessment, with a view to making her airworthy again. In August 1991 she returned to St. Athan where the work is being carrried out.

Spitfire L.F.IXC MK356 seen in May 1961, displayed at Hawkinge in Kent. Within seven months Hawkinge had closed down. "356" was on the move.
(D. H. Fife)

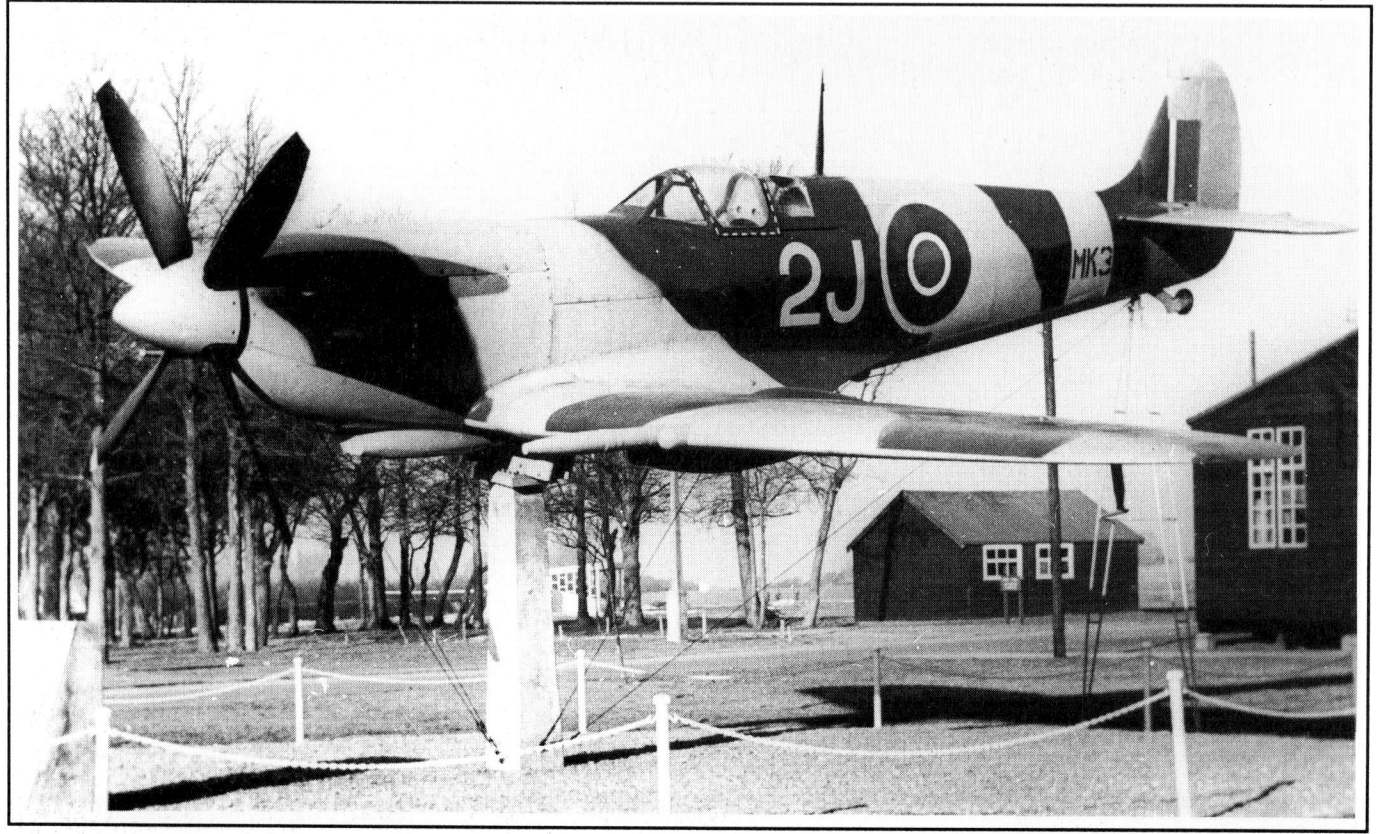

Following restoration at Bicester, MK356 stood guard at Locking, placed on a pylon in a flying attitude, coded 2J, the unit markings of No. 443 (R.C.A.F.) Squadron, with which she flew in 1944.
(Ron W. Cranham)

1970 saw MK356 join the St. Athan Historic Aircraft Collection. Just visible behind the tail is Fiat CR42 Falco MM 5701, which force landed on the shingle beach of Orford Ness in November 1940 and is now displayed in the Battle of Britain Museum, Hendon.
(Ron W. Cranham)

MK356 with invasion stripes in 1988. These were originally applied on the eve of D-Day for ease of recognition, on all allied aircraft flying over Europe.
(Crown Copyright/ M.O.D.)

During 1989 MK356 was moved from St. Athan to Abingdon for a thorough examination with a view to restoration to flying condition and she has now returned to St. Athan for the work to be carried out.
(Neil Randell)

MK732

Spitfire L.F.IXC MK732 was taken on charge by the R.A.F. in March 1944 and issued to No. 485 Squadron R.N.Z.A.F. the following month. This unit was part of the 2nd T.A.F. and during the spring and summer was fighting against both air and ground targets in France. Over the following months it shot down at least one enemy aircraft and shared in the destruction of another. Things did not go all her own way, as in the same period, she suffered three accidents, the last in September 1944. After repair, MK732 was not returned to her Squadron but placed in store. She was one of a batch of Spitfires sold to the R.Neth.A.F., arriving in Holland during June 1948. She was placed in store at Leeuwarden until March 1949, then issued to the Jacht Vlieg School at Twenthe A.F.B. Before the year was out she suffered a flying accident and following repair, MK732 was transferred to No. 322 Squadron at Twenthe, joining them at the end of April 1951. From October 1951 until September 1953 she served with the Leeuwarden Gunnery School but soon afterwards MK732 was taken out of service and issued to Eindhoven A.F.B. as a decoy. The R.A.F. was stationed at Oldenburg in 1956 and a group from No. 14 Squadron acquired this Spitfire in the dead of night! After a quick restoration, she was painted in camouflage scheme and D-Day invasion stripes and put on at this base. This Spitfire later moved briefly to R.A.F. Aldhorn and in 1960, arrived at Gütersloh for display. In June 1969 she returned to England and, after a period in store at St. Athan, MK732 travelled to Bicester, arriving at the end of 1970 and remaining until 1974. She then became a source for spare parts for the B.B.M.F., then based at Coltishal. The Flight's Mk VB AB910 suffered serious damage after being struck by a Harvard at an airshow in Switzerland in August 1978. MK732 was transferred to Abingdon in September 1980, where she donated many parts to the rebuild of this Spitfire. At the same time her tail section was exchanged for some propeller blades, owned by an Australian collector. Behind the scenes, efforts were being made to return MK732 to Holland and in March 1984 she was transferred to Gilze-Rijen A.F.B.

Over the next six years all the necessary parts were located or re-manufactured to allow a rebuild. Work began in 1990 and on 10th June 1993 MK732 took to the air again under her own power for the first time in nearly 30 years. She is now operated by the 'Spitfire Flight' from Deelen and Gilze-Rijen Air Bases, although she is expected to move to Soestorberg in the near future.

MK 732 at Gütersloh in the early 1960's, her canopy had been smashed during a camp dance, until a replacement could be found a cover was strapped over the cockpit.
(Ron W. Cranham)

MK732 was used as a source of spare parts for the B.B.M.F. This picture taken in 1983 shows what remained of this Spitfire before its return to Holland in March 1984.
(*M.A.P.*)
▶

In 1949 MK732 was issued to the Jacht Vlieg (Fighter) School at Twenthe, it was therefore fitting that following her restoration she should once again wear the markings of that unit. Seen here at Lydd in June 1993.
(*Richard H. Paver*)
▶

In June 1994 MK732 is seen at Wroughton painted in No. 485 Squadron markings, looking just as she did while operating over the Normandy Beaches on D-Day, 50 years ago.
(*Neil Randell*)
▶

MK959

Spitfire L.F.IXC MK959 was taken on charge by the R.A.F. in April 1944 joining No. 302 (Poznan) Squadron during early May. Her stay with this Polish unit lasted only a month and in June she was transferred to No. 329 Squadron. After a few days, MK959 was issued to No. 84 Group Support Unit, but early in July it was with No. 3501 Support Unit, awaiting Squadron service. At last, in August 1944, she joined No. 165 "Times of Ceylon" Squadron. This proved to be her last posting of W.W.II., as in February 1945, following an accident, it travelled to Scottish Aviation Ltd., for repair, after which it was placed in store. By the end of September 1946 this Spitfire was sold to the R.Neth.A.F. and flown to Twenthe A.F.B., where it was issued to the Jacht Vlieg School, serving with them until March 1949. MK959 was then overhauled and in 1950 was transferred to No. 322 Squadron, back at Twenthe. By mid July 1954 she had been issued to Volkel for decoy duties but moved to Haarlem for display, but by the end of August she had been transferred to Eindhoven. In 1955 it spent some time on display with No. 315 Squadron R.Neth. A.F. but was then handed over to the R.A.F. at Eindhoven in September, who kept her until October 1961, when they returned to England. In 1964 this Spitfire was mounted on a pylon outside the Officers' Mess. Over the years MK959 has been taken down for restoration and repainting. In more recent times she was moved to Deelan A.F.B. and is currently being offered for sale.

MK959 first arrived at Eindhoven for display in the 1950', we see her in 1964 outside the Officers' Mess. *(Ron W. Cranham)*

▲

For many years this Spitfire was coded VL-V with the serial MJ289 representing an aeroplane of No. 167 Squadron. The real MJ289 failed to return from a "sortie" in April 1945.

(A.P.N.)

In 1946 this Spitfire was issued to the Jacht Vlieg (Fighter) School at Twenthe and coded H-15. She is seen in this picture taken during the late 1980's wearing the markings issued at that time.

(Chris Shelton)

▶

MT847

Spitfire F.R.XIVE MT847 was built in 1945 and placed in store during February, being issued to Boscombe Down in December for use in experimental and development work. She went back into store some time in February 1946 and remained there until November 1950, when joining No. 226 O.C.U. This was to be her first and last R.A.F. unit. MT847 ceased flying in August 1951 and was down-graded for display duties, firstly at Warton, moving on to Freckleton in 1955 and then Middleton St. George.

From 1964 to date this Spitfire has been at Cosford, initially on the parade ground, then placed indoors within the Aerospace Museum.

Spitfire F.R.XIVE MT847 coded MT-E (Medical Training Establishment) at M.T.E. Freckleton circa 1955. Notice the retractable tail wheel, and broad chord fin and rudder designed to counter the torque from the Griffon 65 engine. *(Ron W. Cranham)*

Still in all silver finish, pylon mounted next to the parade ground at Cosford in 1970. This is the only Spitfire Mark XIV still retained by the R.A.F. *(Ron W. Cranham)*

In 1988, now installed in the Aerospace Museum at Cosford. Standing under the wing of a PBY-6A Catalina, formerly with the Royal Danish Air Force. In the foreground a sectionalised Merlin engine, as fitted to early Spitfires. *(Ray C. Coulson)*

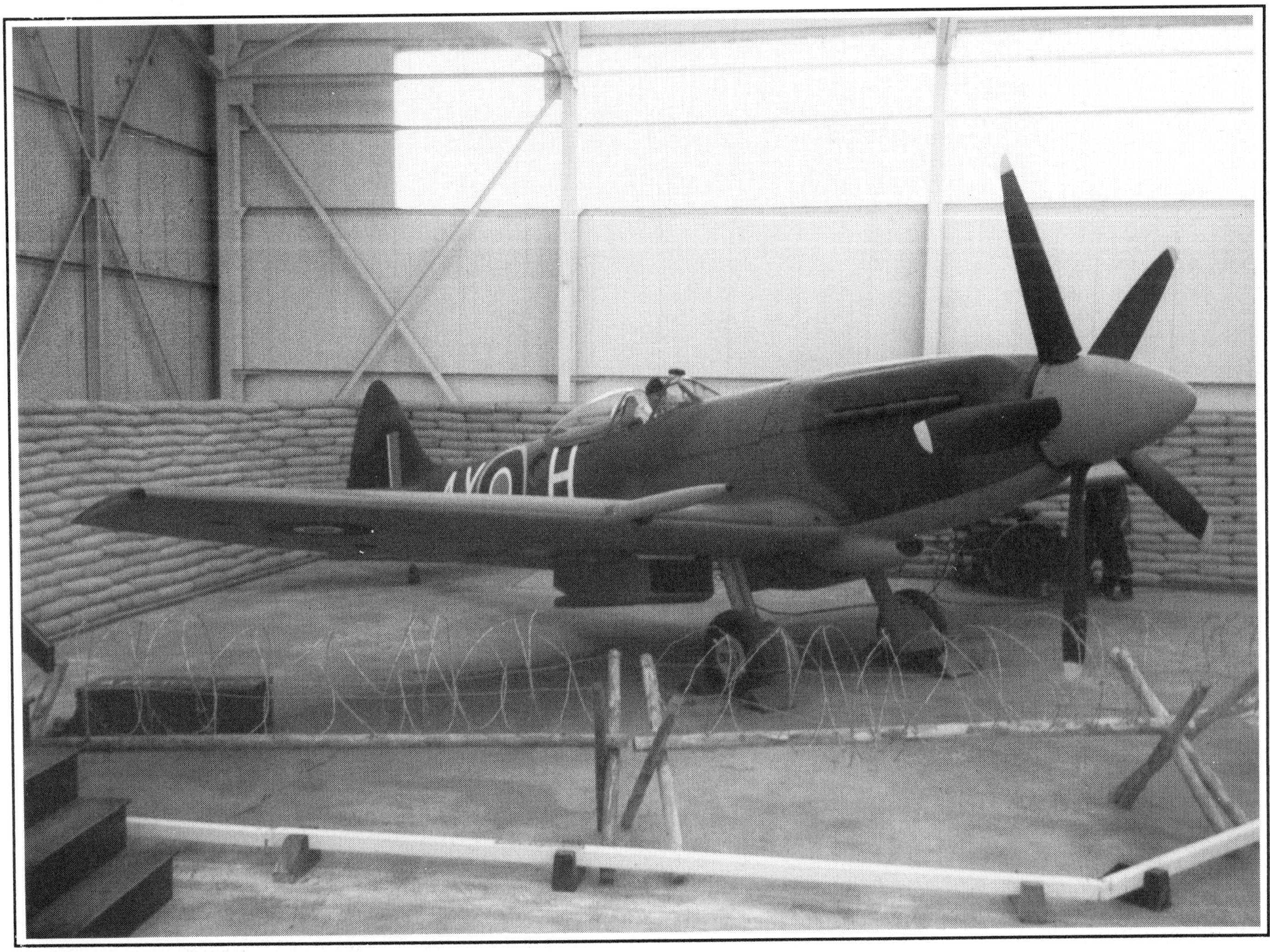

MT847 still at Cosford in 1993. It now sits in a blast pen with her pilot in the cockpit. By pressing a button on the wall her propeller rotates. *(Ray C. Coulson)*

RM694

Spitfire F.XIVC RM694 was taken on charge by the R.A.F. in July 1944 and joined No. 91 (Nigeria) Squadron. In August she was credited with shooting down a VI flying bomb. Later that month she was transferred to No.402 (Winnipeg Bear) Squadron R.C.A.F. and flew with them from bases in Belgium. Following a flying accident she was repaired back in England. July 1945 saw her issued to the C.F.E. at West Raynham, flying with them until November 1948. After suffering another flying accident, RM694 was transferred to No. 5 School of Technical Training in February 1949. Early in 1950 this Spitfire was placed on display at Hornchurch where it remained until the base closed in 1962.

She was sold to a private collector who used her wings on another restoration project. The fuselage is currently thought to be stored by its owner in Florida, U.S.A.

Spitfire F.XIVC RM694, displayed outside the Aircrew Selection Centre at Hornchurch in 1959, carrying her 'M' number 6640M. Of particular interest is the tail unit which makes this Spitfire look quite odd if we compare it to Spitfire MT847. Perhaps while serving as an instructional airframe some years earlier, her tail was replaced with one more befitting an earlier Mark. *(M.A.P.)*

RM694 at Hornchurch in April 1962. Soon Hornchurch would close and once removed, "694" would never be seen on display again. *(Ron W. Cranham)*

RM694 on the camp dump at R.A.F. Bicester. She was bought by a business man who moved her to his garage in Cheshire.
(Ron W. Cranham)

The owner at that time, Mr. A. H. Brookes, poses with his Spitfire.
(Daily Express)

RR263

Spitfire L.F. XVIE RR263 was taken on charge by the R.A.F. in October 1944. She flew with No. 66 Squadron, joining them at Grimbergen in Belgium, as part of the 2nd Tactical Air Force, until April 1945. In June of the same year she was transferred to No. 416 (City of Oshawa) Squadron and flew with them until late October. Then followed a long period in store until November 1949, when she was used for test work by Vickers-Armstrong, returning to store a few weeks later. She flew with No. 4 C.A.A.C.U. at Llandow in Wales from August 1951 until July 1954 and was then placed in store. Eventually RR263 went on display at Kenley in 1955, where she remained until May 1967 when it was decided to donate her to the French Air Force. Soon she could be seen at Tours Air Base and in 1978 this Spitfire moved to the Musée de L'Air et de L'Espace at Le Bourget where she can still be seen.

Spitfire L. F. XVIE RR263 seen in March 1961 at R.A.F. Kenley, wearing the codes issued to her while serving with No. 66 Squadron during World War II. Her colour scheme at this time was a very inappropriate brown and green. *(Ron W. Cranham)*

In 1967 RR263 was presented to the French Air Force as a Memorial to the Free French pilots who flew with the R.A.F. Seen now at the entrance to Tours Air Base, a gate she guarded until 1976, re-serialised as TB597. *(Musée de L'Air et de L'Espace)*

Following restoration, RR263 was put on display at the Musee de L'Air et de L'Espace. Still in her fictitious markings, the real TB597 failed to return from an 'Operation' on 1st April 1945, while flying with No. 340 (Ile de France) Squadron.

(Musée de L'Air et de L'Espace)

RW382

Spitfire L.F.XVIE RW382 was taken on charge by the R.A.F. in July 1945. With the war over, there was no rush to get her into Squadron use, so she was stored until April 1947. RW382 was then issued to No. 604 (County of Middlesex) Squadron R.Aux.A.F. and flew with them until April 1950. She then went back into store for just over a year and in June 1951 was transferred briefly to No. 3 C.A.A.C.U. Her final move came four months later, when she arrived at the Control and Reporting School, Middle Wallop. She finally ceased flying in July 1953 and was eventually put on display at Church Fenton. 1959 saw her transferred to Leconfield where she remained until 1967 when she was taken to Henlow for use in the film "The Battle of Britain". After the film, she was restored at Kemble, eventually being issued to Uxbridge in 1973. RW382 was part of the R.A.F./H.F.L. exchange deal and as such left Uxbridge during 1988. Her restoration to flying condition began and she took to the air again in July 1991. Today RW382 is still operating from the H.F.L. airfield on behalf of her owner.

RW382 coded NG-C while operating with No. 604 (County of Middlesex) Squadron from Hendon, circa 1947.
(F. K. Griffiths/Peter R. Arnold Collection)

Spitfire L.F.XVIE RW382 while displayed at Church Fenton circa 1955. The markings are those of a Fighter Command Control and Reporting School, Middle Wallop, a unit she flew with in 1952. In place of her serial number, we see her 'M' number, issued when she was down-graded from flying to instructional airframe use.
(A.P.N.)

RW382 at Henlow in 1967 after her arrival from Leconfield for use in the film "The Battle of Britain". Although not clearly visible in this shot, "382" carried the false serial RW729 and coded AZ-B of No. 234 Squadron.
(Ron W. Cranham)

RW382 at Uxbridge during the summer of 1985, this Spitfire remained on display at this Station for almost fifteen years.
(Neil Randell)

RW382 remained at Uxbridge until 1988 when she was involved in the R.A.F./H.F.L. exchange deal. She was the first of the H.F.L. Spitfires to be restored, flying again by mid 1991. Pictured here in the summer of 1993 at Duxford.
(Ron W. Cranham)

RW386

Spitfire L.F.XVIE RW386 was taken on charge by the R.A.F. in August 1945 and stored until March 1947, when she was issued to No. 604 (County of Middlesex) Squadron. By 1952 she had ceased flying and become an instructional airframe and was transferred to Honington. Late 1957 saw RW386 move to Halton where she was displayed until finally passing to St. Athan in 1980. During 1982 she was part of an exchange deal and so moved to War Birds of Great Britain at their Biggin Hill home. RW386 was moved to H.F.L. in September 1991 for restoration, but before completion was transferred to Florida, U.S.A., and is awaiting a decision on her future.

Spitfire L.F.XVIE RW386 in 1957 at Halton now down-graded to an instructional airframe. Notice the engine cowling, the lack of exhaust stack suggests that this Spitfire may be engineless! *(M.A.P.)*

RW386 at Halton in 1965. Of interest are the exhaust stubs, which would be better suited to another type. Although not a Gate Guard in the strictest sense, it was the Station mascot and displayed outside on Open Days. *(Ron W. Cranham)*

RW386 at St. Athan in 1981, in the markings she wore whilst with No. 604 (County of Middlesex) Squadron R.Aux.A.F. in the late 1940's. Included in an exchange in 1982 for a Sopwith "Pup" replica, which went to the R.A.F. Museum, Hendon, this Spitfire joined the growing collection of aeroplanes owned by W.B. of G.B. at Biggin Hill. *(M.A.P.)*

Pictured at Audley End in late 1992, although restoration was virtually complete, prior to final assembly, RW386 was transferred to the U.S.A. *(Richard H. Paver)*

RW388

Spitfire L.F.XVIE RW388 was taken on charge by the R.A.F. in July 1945 and joined No. 667 Squadron the following month. She had an accident later that year and following repairs was stored until June 1949 when she was issued to No. 5 Squadron. During April 1951 she spent a few days with No. 612 Squadron before her final move, transferring to the Fighter Command Control and Reporting School at Middle Wallop. Following a flying accident in January 1952 she never flew again but was issued to Colerne for display purposes. During the 1960's RW388 went on to be displayed at Benson and Andover. Eventually she was given to the City of Stoke-on-Trent, birthplace of her designer, R. J. Mitchell, going on display early in 1972. Today she can be seen in the City Museum.

Spitfire L.F.XVIE RW388 seen at Farnborough in 1945, whilst flying with No. 667 Anti-Aircraft Squadron, coded U4-U.
(Peter R. Arnold Collection)

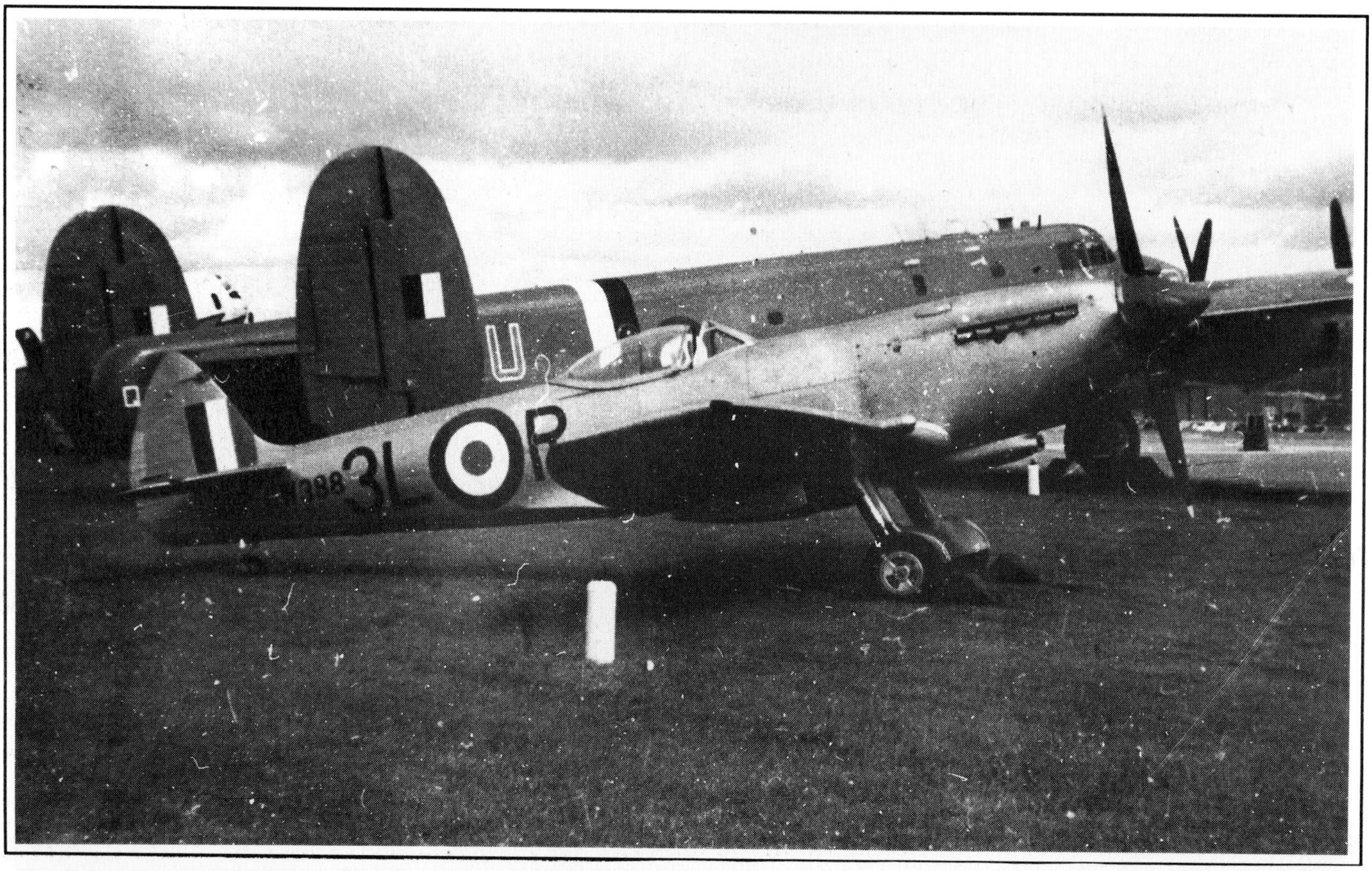

Her flying days over, RW388 on display at Colerne in September 1957. Like a lot of display Spitfires, still carrying the markings of her last Squadron, the F.C.C. & R.S.
(Chris J. Foulds/Ray C. Coulson)

In the 1960's on the gate of Andover, unlike so many other Spitfires, she was not used in the film "The Battle of Britain" but had been converted into an earlier Mark for use in the 1968 Royal Tournament. *(Ron W. Cranham)*

In 1972 RW388 was presented to the City of Stoke-on-Trent, the birthplace of her designer, R. J. Mitchell. She was moved inside the City Museum and Art Gallery in 1985. *(The City of Stoke-on-Trent Museum and Art Gallery/Richard Weston)*

RW393

Spitfire L.F.XVIE RW393 was taken on charge by the R.A.F. in July 1945 and stored until November 1947. She was then issued to No. 203 A.F.S., remaining until early 1948 when she moved to the Fighter Command Control and Reporting School at Middle Wallop. During 1950 RW393 became the personal mount of the A.O.C. Fighter Command Air Marshal Sir William Elliot. She was looked after by No. 31 (Metropolitan Communications Flight) Squadron, and painted in an all white scheme with a red flash on both sides of the fuselage, made up with red crosses. RW393 remained with No. 31 Squadron until October 1953, when she was transferred to No. 3 C.A.A.C.U. at Exeter, where her flying days ended in July 1954. She was issued to Turnhouse for display during early 1957, remaining there until 1989.

In accordance with Government policy, RW393 was removed from outside display and placed in store at St. Athan, where she remains to this day.

Spitfire L.F. XVIE RW393 at R.A.F. Odiham in 1949, painted white, the personal mount of Air Marshal Sir William Elliot, who was A.O.C. Fighter Command. *(Crown Copyright/R.A.F.M.)*

RW393 arrived at Turnhouse for display in 1957. She is seen in 1959 in the markings of a No. 603 (City of Edinburgh) Squadron R.Aux.A.F. aircraft. *(M.A.P.)*

RW393 outside the Headquarters for R.A.F. Turnhouse in September 1988. Following the decision to remove all Spitfire Gate Guards, she was transferred to St. Athan in 1989. *(Crown Copyright/M.O.D.)*

Enjoying the sun at St. Athan in February 1990. Of the seven Spitfires stored there, she has the most internally intact cockpit, still having most of her instruments, gun sight and seat. *(Ray C. Coulson)*

SL542

Spitfire L.F.XVIE SL542 was taken on charge by the R.A.F. in July 1945, the following month she was issued to No. 595 Squadron and flew with them until July 1948. She was then transferred to No. 695 Squadron and remained until December 1950. SL542 moved once again, this time joining No. 1 C.A.A.C.U., serving with them until July 1951, after which she was placed in store, being taken on by No. 2 C.A.A.C.U. in March 1954. This Spitfire suffered a flying accident in January 1957 and never flew again. She was initially displayed at Duxford and then passed on to Horsham St. Faith in 1962. When this station closed in 1963 she moved to Coltishall, remaining on display until December 1988. Next came a period in store at St. Athan and then, in 1992, she was exchanged for a Handley Page Hampden bomber which will eventually go on display at the R.A.F.M. SL542 is now in the U.S.A. for restoration.

Spitfire L.F.XVIE SL542 in 1948, flying with No. 695 Squadron and coded 4M-N. Her flying career came to an end following a flying accident at Duxford in January 1957.
(Peter H. T. Green Collection)

Duxford, circa 1960, SL542 in the markings of a No. 64 Squadron aircraft. The other side was coded "YT-N", the markings of a No. 65 Squadron aircraft. The hangar behind SL542 was destroyed for special effect during the making of the film "The Battle of Britain". All that remains is the base!
(Ron W. Cranham)

May 1962. Duxford had closed and we see SL542 transferred to Horsham-St. Faith and mounted on a pylon. Slung between two radiators is a 45 gallon drop tank.
(Ron W. Cranham)

SL542 spent a total of 22 years at Coltishall. Seen here after a new paint job in 1985, carrying the codes, once again, which she wore while flying with No. 695 Squadron during the late 1940's.
(Ray C. Coulson)

SL574

Spitfire L.F.XVIE SL574 was taken on charge by the R.A.F. in August 1945 and placed in store until September 1947. She then joined the Empire Air Armament School and flew with them until July 1949. For the next four months SL574 flew with the C.G.S. but in November went back into store. April 1951 saw her issued to No. 102 F.R.S., staying until October, then back into store, transferring to No. 3 C.A.A.C.U. in October 1953. She was selected as an airworthy Spitfire to appear in the film "Reach For The Sky" and left her unit briefly late in 1955 and joined the other Spitfires for the flying sequences of the film. SL574 later rejoined her unit where she remained until June 1956. Following a period in store, and used for ground display, she was selected to join the Memorial Flight (the forerunner of The Battle of Britain Memorial Flight) in 1957. A forced landing on a cricket pitch in September 1959 brought her flying days to an end and following repair SL574 was put on display at Bentley Priory. She moved to Henlow during 1967 to join other Spitfires being used in the film "The Battle of Britain", returning to Bentley Priory in late 1969. This Spitfire remained at Bentley until 1986, when she left for Halton where she was restored prior to leaving for the U.S.A., where she is now displayed at the San Diego Aerospace Museum.

Spitfire L.F.XVIE SL574 is seen during September 1947 when serving with the Empire Air Armament School at Manby and coded FG-CU.
(A. S. Thomas/Peter H. T. Green Collection)

This Spitfire began her role as a display aeroplane at Bentley Priory, this picture shows her soon after arriving in August 1961.
(Ron W. Cranham)

May 1973, still at Bentley Priory, coded AZ-B (No. 234 Squadron) perhaps in recognition of the aircraft of this Squadron who were under the control of No. 11 Group (Bentley Priory) during the early war years.
(Ron W. Cranham)

SL574 nearing the end of her restoration at Halton by volunteers of No. 2 Wing and other trainees from No. 1 S.T.T.
(Steven J. Chamberlain)

Now displayed in cramped conditions at the San Diego Aerospace Museum as a tribute to the American pilots who flew with the R.A.F. It is painted to represent a Spitfire of No. 133 Eagle Squadron.
(Peter Arnold Collection)

SL674

Spitfire L.F.XVIE SL674 was taken on charge by the R.A.F. in July 1945 but was not issued until April 1946, going to No. 17 O.T.U., where she stayed until October and subsequently went back into store. August 1947 saw SL674 transferred to No. 501 Squadron, suffering a landing accident in September 1948. Following repair, in November she was returned to her unit until being issued to No. 612 (County of Aberdeen) Squadron R.Aux.A.F. in April 1949, remaining on squadron strength until July 1951. This Spitfire returned to store but was chosen to go on display at the Memorial Chapel, Biggin Hill. Her final flight was in September 1954, when she flew to Biggin Hill and joined Hurricane LF738 outside the chapel. SL674 remained on display until being removed to St. Athan in March 1989, where she remains in store.

Spitfire L.F.XVIE SL674, while serving with No. 501 Squadron, suffered a landing accident at Filton on 4th September, 1948. She is seen with a recovery crew in attendance soon afterwards. *(Peter R. Arnold Collection)*

April 1961 and SL674 after a much needed paint job, guarding the gate of the Memorial Chapel at Biggin Hill. *(Ron W. Cranham)*

Perhaps with thoughts of Biggin Hill during the Battle of Britain, SL674 inappropriately painted in 1940 scheme, circa 1986.
(Neil Randell)

1988 and more accurate paintwork and Squadron markings had been applied, once again wearing her codes of the late 1940's while flying with No. 612 (County of Aberdeen) Squadron.
(Ray C. Coulson)

SM411

Spitfire L.F.XVIE SM411 was taken on charge by the R.A.F. in November 1944. She flew with No. 421 (Red Indian) Squadron R.C.A.F., operating from airfields in Belgium and Germany. After the war she returned to the U.K. and went into store. Between April and October of 1951, SM411 served with No. 102 and No. 103 Flying Refresher Schools, then once again went back into store. She was issued to No. 3 C.A.A.C.U. in October 1953 but ceased flying in May 1954. Her next move was to Wattisham for display purposes, remaining there until 1967, when she was taken to Henlow for use in the film "The Battle of Britain". Following the film SM411 was restored and in 1971 she joined the R.A.F. Exhibition Flight at Abingdon. In the late 1970's this Spitfire was part of an exchange deal, and moved to Poland and is currently displayed in the Muzeum Lotnictwa Astronautyki.

Spitfire L.F.XVIE SM411, looking very clean in her all silver finish in 1960. In the mid-1950s she began her role of display aircraft at Wattisham and was to remain there for the next 12 years.
(Ron W. Cranham)

In the codes of a No. 695 Squadron aircraft SM411 is seen in a hangar at Henlow in 1967, being prepared for use in the film "The Battle of Britain". She was brought up to taxiing condition by Simpsons Aero Services.
(Ron W. Cranham)

Following her film role, it was decided to send SM411 to No. 71 M.U. at Bicester. She is seen being prepared for use with the R.A.F. Exhibition Flight in August 1971. The markings are those of No. 421 Squadron R.C.A.F., a unit she flew with in World War II.
(Peter Arnold Collection)

SM411 at the Muzeum Lotnictwa Astronautyki, Krakow. She was swapped in 1975 for a DH9A which is now at the R.A.F. Museum, Hendon.
(Crown copyright/M.O.D. via Muzeum Lotnictwa Astronautyki)

TB252

Spitfire L.F.XVIE TB252 was taken on charge by the R.A.F. in January 1945, joining No. 329 Squadron in March, flying as part of the 2nd T.A.F. Soon afterwards she was damaged and following repair, a week later was allocated to No. 341 (Alsace) Squadron. She flew with them from bases in Holland until the end of the war. In January 1946 TB252 was transferred to No. 350 (Belgium) Squadron and flew with them until October 1946. She joined her final operational unit, No. 61 O.T.U., arriving in May 1947, but by early 1949 she was surplus to requirements and stored. During 1955 TB252 was issued to Odiham as an instructional airframe, remaining until late 1959. She then transferred to Acklington for display for the next ten years, before moving to Boulmer. From here, this Spitfire went on to be exhibited at Leuchars, making her final move in 1986. Her home was to be Bentley Priory, replacing SL674. TB252 was part of the R.A.F./H.F.L. exchange deal and was removed from display in 1989. She is currently being restored to flying condition at Audley End.

Spitfire L.F.XVIE TB252 seen during 1946 while flying with No. 350 (Belgium) Squadron in Europe. *(Peter R. Arnold Collection)*

TB252 was issued to Acklington for display in 1959. Seen here in 1963. Somewhere along the way she has lost her tail wheel.
(Ron W. Cranham)

TB252 at Leuchars in 1972, now sporting the markings of a Spitfire which flew with No. 340 'Ile de France' Squadron, from bases in Holland.
(Ron W. Cranham)

If the tree in the background looks familiar, it should, we are back at Bentley Priory. TB252 had been brought here as a replacement for SL574 which was going to the U.S.A. In 1989 this Spitfire was part of the R.A.F./H.F.L. exchange deal.
(Chris Shelton)

TB252 in store at the H.F.L. hangar at Audley End, prior to restoration.
(Ray C. Coulson)

TB382

Spitfire L.F.XVIE TB382 was taken on charge by the R.A.F. in January 1945. In February she joined No. 602 (County of Glasgow) Squadron R.Aux.A.F., taking part in fighter-bomber and dive-bombing missions on targets in Holland and North-West Germany. After the war TB382 was stored, then in January 1949 she was issued to Fighter Command Communication Flight at Northolt. Her flying career ended in May 1951 following a flying accident. After repair there followed a long period in store until she was selected for display at Thornaby in 1955. This Spitfire then moved to Middleton-St. George in August 1956 and continued in her new role. TB382 remained until 1965 and then passed on to Ely. Like many other Spitfires, 1967 saw her move to Henlow for use in the film "The Battle of Britain". Filming over, TB382 was issued to the Exhibition Flight at Abingdon, joining them during 1969, where she remains as part of the Flight.

Spitfire TB382 although located at Middleton-St. George is seen here on a return visit to Thornaby on Battle of Britain Day 1956. The crest on the engine cowling is that of No. 608 Squadron.
(Richard S. Fell)

Middleton-St. George circa 1960 now sporting a camouflage scheme and her "M" number has been retained in place of her serial number.
(A.P.N.)

In May 1965 TB382 began her final posting as a display aircraft at the R.A.F. Hospital, Ely. She is wearing the markings first issued to her whilst serving with No. 604 Squadron in early 1945. *(Ron W. Cranham)*

In 1969 TB382 joined the R.A.F. Exhibition Flight and is seen fulfilling this role at Horse Guards Parade in September 1990. Her markings represent those of a No. 603 Squadron aircraft, which flew from Hornchurch in September 1940. *(Ron W. Cranham)*

TB752

Spitfire L.F.XVIE TB752 was taken on charge by the R.A.F. in February 1945. She was delivered to No. 66 Squadron in late March and was soon in action flying from bases in Holland. TB752 was damaged in an accident at the end of March and following repairs was allocated to No. 403 (Wolf) Squadron R.C.A.F. in April. At that time they were operating from bases in Germany. By the end of the war, this Spitfire is credited with shooting down at least four enemy aircraft. On her return to England she was put into store, emerging in April 1951 and flying for the next 28 months with No. 102 and No. 103 F.R.S. In November 1953 she was transferred to No. 5 C.A.A.C.U., serving with them until November 1954. TB752 ceased flying in 1955 and was placed on display at Manston. After spending almost 25 years being displayed at the mercy of our ever-changing weather, she underwent a restoration and was installed in a purpose-built memorial building, where she has been since 1980.

A fine study of TB752 taken while serving with No. 403 (Canadian) Squadron by her pilot Flt. Lt. C. L. Rispler in Holland, early 1945.
(C. L. Rispler/Lewis E. Deal)

Although a poor quality picture, it shows TB752 at Hawarden circa 1954 coded 'F' of No. 5 C.A.A.C.U. *(Chris J. Foulds/Ray C. Coulson)*

TB752 guarding the gate at Manston in 1957, still in a silver scheme.
(A.P.N.)

Following restoration by the Medway Branch of the Aeronautical Society in 1980, TB752 was finished in the markings issued to her whilst serving with No. 66 Squadron in March 1945.
(Ron W. Cranham)

In this picture taken in 1994, we can see a sample of the stores she could carry, which included either two 250lb., bombs or one 500lb., bomb.
(Crown Copyright/MOD/ P. Crouch)

TD135

Spitfire L.F.XVIE TD135 was taken on charge by the R.A.F. in March 1945. In May she was issued to the A.F.D.S. of the C.F.E., her stay lasting nearly two years. March 1947 saw her transferred to No. 604 (County of Middlesex) Squadron, which was to be her last flying unit. She suffered a flying accident in November 1950 and was relegated to display duties, travelling to No. 346 (South Shields) Squadron Air Training Corps.. in Preston. By 1963 she was in a very sorry state and moved to the dump at Dishforth, being sold by tender for a mere £25! Soon TD135 could be seen on display outside a public house appropriately called "The Spitfire Inn". In the mid 1970's she was sold and is currently under restoration in Genesio State, New York, U.S.A.

Spitfire L.F.XVIE TD135, unlike most guards, was issued to an Air Training Corps Unit No. 346 (South Shields) Squadron. She is pictured circa 1957, in all silver finish with the codes of No. 604 (County of Middlesex) Squadron R.Aux.A.F., a unit she served with during the late 1940's.
(M.A.P.)

A rather sad looking TD135, still with No. 346 Squadron ATC in 1963. Soon after this picture was taken she was moved to the dump at Dishforth and was sold by tender for £25!
(Ron W. Cranham)

Her new owner restored TD135 and put her on display outside his pub in Herefordshire, circa 1972. She is fitted with an odd looking propeller, her original one being removed whilst at Dishforth and used in the restoration of MkV EP120. *(Ron W. Cranham)*

TD135 in the U.S.A., tucked away in the back of a hanger at Elkhart Airfield, Indiana in October 1979. Now, 15 years later and away from the public's gaze, work continues to bring this Spitfire back to airworthy condition. *(Peter R. Arnold Collection)*

TD248

Spitfire L.F.XVIE TD248 was taken on charge by the R.A.F. in May 1945, and was issued to No. 695 Squadron in July, serving with them until 1951. She transferred to No. 2 C.A.A.C.U. during August 1951 and served with them for the next three years. TD248 ceased flying in May 1954 and was eventually posted to Hooton Park for display in October 1955. In April 1959 she was issued to No. 1336 Squadron, A.T.C., and moved to Sealand for display, remaining until November 1988, when she was removed as part of the R.A.F./H.F.L. exchange deal. Her restoration to flying condition began in 1990 and TD248 took to the air again during November 1992. She now operates from Earls Colne in Essex.

Spitfire L.F.XVIE TD248 was put on display at Hooton Park in October 1955. With the disbandment of the R. Aux.A.F. she was moved into store there pending her next move in July 1959. *(Chris J. Foulds)*

At Sealand in June 1967. Because of its poor condition the canopy has been painted silver. *(Chris J. Foulds)*

By November 1988, TD248 had been displayed at Sealand for over 20 years. This picture shows her on the day she was to be taken down, being part of the R.A.F./H.F.L. exchange deal. *(Eddie K. Coventry)*

Her restoration to flying condition did not begin until 1990. By September 1992 it was almost complete. TD248 flew again on 10th November 1992. Her colour scheme depicts a Spitfire flown by No. 41 Squadron from Wittering during 1946. *(Ray C. Coulson)*

TE184

Spitfire L.F.XVIE TE184 was taken on charge by the R.A.F. in May 1945 and placed in store until July 1947, when she was issued to No. 203 A.F.S., renamed No. 226 O.C.U. in June 1949, flying with them until February 1950. TE184 was then transferred to No. 607 (County of Durham) Squadron R.Aux.A.F. for a short time, and by November she had moved to the C.G.S. at Leconfield. This proved to be her last operational unit. Following a flying accident in January 1951, TE184 was relegated to instructional airframe status and issued to No. 64 Reserve Centre at Long Benton. Her first posting as a display aircraft came in 1952 with a transfer to No. 1855 Squadron (A.T.C.) at Royston, where she remained until 1967, when she moved to Finningley. It was decided to donate this Spitfire to the Ulster Folk and Transport Museum in Northern Ireland. During 1970, restoration work was carried out at Kemble, prior to her departure from the mainland. First came a long period in store, then she was placed on display in 1977 and remained with the museum until 1986, when, as part of an exchange deal she returned to be restored to flying condition. However, her shape was to change, her cutback fuselage and teardrop canopy being replaced by the earlier, more traditional, Spitfire style. TE184 is now airworthy following first test flight in November 1990 and operates from Jersey in the Channel Isles with her owners Myrick Aviation.

Spitfire L.F.XVIE TE184 was issued for display in the early 1950's to No. 1855 (A.T.C.) Squadron at Royston, Lancashire. This picture shows a shabby looking aircraft during 1957. She still carries the codes issued to her while flying with the C.G.S. at Leconfield in 1950. *(T. Fairclough/Ray C. Coulson)*

TE184 at Finningley in 1968. Her new found codes (standing for Mechanical Engineering 'M' Squadron) were applied while she was loaned to Cranwell for a dance. The artwork on the nose was applied when '184' was used in a television programme. *(Chris Shelton)*

During the early 1970's TE184 was given to the Ulster Folk and Transport Museum. She is seen here during a brief spell outside coded LA-A.
(Thomas Maddock/Alan Watson)

In 1986 TE184 left the Ulster Museum and in 1988 moved to Trent Aero to be rebuilt as a high back Mark XVIE for her owners Myrick Aviation. By April 1990 the transformation, as we can see in this picture, is quite dramatic.
(Peter R. Arnold Collection)

This Spitfire, now painted in P.R.U. colours, flew during the 50th Anniversary of D-Day Airshow at Duxford in June 1994. During the day she encountered engine problems and as a result remained at Duxford after the show for repairs.
(Richard H. Paver)

TE214

Spitfire L.F.XVIE TE214 was taken on charge by the R.A.F. in April 1945, and placed in store. She was issued to the C.G.S. in July, flying with them from Leconfield until a flying accident in March 1950 ended her flying days. After repair she eventually transferred to Ternhill for display. In 1960 this Spitfire was sent to Canada, moving over the years from the Canadian War Museum in Ottawa to the West Canadian Aviation Museum, arriving at the latter in December 1988.

Spitfire L.F.VXIE TE214 was something of a camp mascot, only appearing on display at open days. This picture shows her at R.A.F. Ternhill during the late 1950's carrying the false serial TE353.
(Ron W. Cranham)

She was transferred to the R.C.A.F. in 1960 and restored to represent a Spitfire of No. 416 (City of Oshawa) Squadron in 1966 and correctly serialised TE214.
(National Aviation Museum, Canada)

This Spitfire transferred to the Western Canada Aviation Museum on long term loan from The National Aviation Museum of Canada, and is seen in the summer of 1990. *(Beverly Tallon, Photographer, Western Canada Aviation Museum/Norma Riordan)*

TE214 seen here in 1993, she remains on display at the W.C.A.M., framed by a rare Junkers W34 Airliner which once flew with Canadian Airlines Limited. *(Peter R. Arnold Collection)*

TE288

Spitfire L.F.XVIE TE288 was taken on charge by the R.A.F. in June 1945 and stored until some time in 1946, when she was issued to No. 61 O.T.U. Her next posting was to No. 502 (County of Gloucester) Squadron R.Aux.A.F., arriving in November 1948 and remaining until March 1949, when once again TE288 was stored. April 1951 saw her move to No. 102 F.R.S. which turned out to be her final operational unit, as she was withdrawn from flying six months later. She went back into store but was chosen to appear in the film "Reach for the Sky". Late in 1955, she was transferred to Rufforth for display duties. In 1959 she moved to Church Fenton, then on to Dishforth, and in 1962 she travelled to New Zealand and was displayed outside the Brevet Club in Canterbury in 1964. Her final home was the R.N.Z.A.F. Museum, at Wigram Air Base, where she can currently be seen.

Although no contemporary photograph is known to exist of this Spitfire while displayed at Rufforth and Church Fenton, we do have this picture showing her displayed away from home, outside York Castle during the 1961 Battle of Britain week. *(Peter R. Arnold Collection)*

In the early 1960's TE288 was given to the Brevet Club in Canterbury, New Zealand and in seen there, circa 1965. *(Ron W. Cranham)*

TE288 following restoration in the 1980's and finished in the markings of a No. 485 (R.N.Z.A.F.) Squadron Spitfire, flown by New Zealand Ace Johnnie Houlton, circa 1986. *(R.N.Z.A.F.M.)*

An interesting setting for TE288, like so many aircraft operating from jungle airstrips in the Far East, she is hidden away from the prying eyes of the enemy under camouflage netting. Her pilot looks on as the armourer cleans one of the cannon barrels. *(Peter R. Arnold Collection)*

TE311

Spitfire L.F.XVIE TE311 was taken on charge by the R.A.F. in June 1945 and was issued to the E.C.F.S. Handling Squadron in October, remaining there until February 1946, when she was placed in store. May 1951 saw her join No. 1689 F.P.T. Flight, flying with them for just over a year. TE311 left in July 1952 and had a brief spell with Flying Training Command. This Spitfire was taken on by the F.T.U. at Benson in April 1953, remaining with them until September, when she was placed in store. Her final operational unit was No. 2 C.A.A.C.U., joining them in January 1954, but the following month was stored again. In 1955 TE311 was issued to Tangmere for display purposes. Her stay lasted almost 12 years, then in 1967 she moved to Henlow for use in the film "The Battle of Britain". After filming she was issued to Benson for display but by 1970 she had been transferred to the Exhibition Flight at Abingdon where she is currently serving with them.

Spitfire L.F.XVIE TE311 in all silver finish on the gate at Tangmere in 1963. In 1967 she was removed to Henlow, being restored to taxiing condition to take part in the film "The Battle of Britain". *(Ron W. Cranham)*

Following filming TE311 was restored, painted in camouflage scheme and displayed on the gate of Benson (July 1971). We can see that 'A' type roundel has been applied under the wings instead of the correct 'C' type, to conform with the rest of the scheme.

(Ron W. Cranham)

During 1970 TE311 was transferred from Benson to Abingdon, so joining the R.A.F. Exhibition Flight. She was taking the place of SM411 which had gone to Poland. 24 years later and TE311 is still fulfilling this role at Abingdon. She has been painted to represent a Spitfire flown by No. 19 Squadron in 1940.

(Neil Randell)

TE356

Spitfire L.F.XVIE TE356 was taken on charge by the R.A.F. in June 1945. The following month she joined No. 695 Squadron (renumbered No. 34 Squadron in February 1949), serving with them until August 1951. TE356 was then transferred to No. 2 C.A.A.C.U. Her flying days ended in September 1952 and she was placed on display at Bicester. In 1967, like so many other Spitfires, TE356 moved to Henlow for use in the film "The Battle of Britain". Following the film, she went on to be displayed at Little Rissington, transferring to Leeming in 1978. TE356 was part of an exchange deal and moved to W.B. of G.B. in 1986. Her restoration to flying condition began and she took to the air again in December 1987. She now flies from Pinal Air Park in Arizona, U.S.A.

Spitfire L.F.XVIE TE356 in April 1961, guarding the parade ground at Bicester, a duty she first began in the early 1950's. Her markings are those issued to her whilst with No. 695 Squadron in the 1940's.
(Ron W. Cranham)

In 1967 TE356 joined the cast of "The Battle of Britain" and was restored to taxiing condition. Following the film it was restored, then issued to Little Rissington in April 1973.
(Ron W. Cranham)

TE356 moved to Leeming in the late 1970's, where she stayed until exchanged for a P47D Thunderbolt in 1986, thus joining the Warbirds of Great Britain collection.
(Alan M. Hewitt)
▶

TE356 under restoration to flying condition at Trent Aero in 1987.
(Ian King)
▶

TE356 at Biggin Hill in 1989 in the codes of her owner at the time, D. Arnold. In early January 1990 she left the U.K. going to the U.S.A.
(Ron W. Cranham)
▶

TE384

Spitfire L.F.XVIE TE384 was taken on charge by the R.A.F. in August 1945 and stored until May 1947, when she was issued to No. 603 (City of Edinburgh) Squadron R.Aux.A.F. In November 1948 she passed on to No. 501 (County of Gloucester) Squadron briefly, as, in March 1949, TE384 was transferred to No. 612 (County of Aberdeen) Squadron. In the early 1950's she was moved to Airwork General Trading Ltd., for an overhaul and on completion was stored until 1954. The following year saw her relegated to display duties and issued to Wymeswold. From there she moved to Syerston, remaining until 1967 when she travelled to Henlow for appearance in the film "The Battle of Britain". After the film TE384 was placed in store until 1972, when she travelled to Australia as part of an exchange deal. After spending several years in store, restoration began in 1983 and she took to the air in October 1988. She now operates from an airfield in Queensland, Australia.

Spitfire L.F.XVIE TE384 during the 1959 Battle of Britain Day at Syerston. *(M.A.P.)*

By the early 1960's TE384 could be seen displayed on the gate at Syerston, looking somewhat like a giant plastic model.

(Ron W. Cranham)

TE384, circa 1964, in the markings of a No. 603 (City of Edinburgh) Squadron R.Aux.A.F. aircraft, a unit she flew with in the 1940's.
(M.A.P.)

TE384 left the U.K. for Australia in 1972. We see her after a lengthy rebuild to flying condition at Toowoomba airfield in April 1988.
(Chris Du Vé/Peter R. Arnold Collection)

TE392

Spitfire L.F.XVIE TE392 was taken on charge by the R.A.F. in June 1945 and placed in store. Eventually she was issued to No. 126 Squadron in March 1946, later passing on to No. 65 Squadron, who shared the same base. She was transferred to No. 164 Squadron in August 1946, flying with them until December 1947. TE392 then joined No. 63 Squadron, remaining until May 1948, when she passed to No. 595 Squadron. July saw her move to No. 695 Squadron and in February the following year the unit was renumbered, becoming No. 34 Squadron. She continued to serve with them until August 1951. Now came her final operational move, transferring to No. 2 C.A.A.C.U. TE392 suffered a flying accident in September 1952 and, following repairs, was issued to Church Lawford for display. Over the next few years this Spitfire could be seen on display at Wellesbourne Mountford, Waterbeach, Kemble and finally Credenhill. In 1984 she was exchanged for a B-25J Mitchell, supplied by W.B. of G.B., and placed in store with them. She is now stored in Florida, U.S.A. awaiting a decision on her future.

Spitfire L.F.XVIE TE392 seen, circa 1957, in silver finish at Wellesbourne Mountford *(Ron W. Cranham)*

TE392, still at Wellesbourne in April 1961 in the markings of No. 65 (East Indian) Squadron, a unit she flew with in the 1940's.
(Ron W. Cranham)

Following the closure of Wellesbourne it was transferred to Kemble and mounted on a pylon during 1967.
(M.A.P.)

This Spitfire was issued to Credenhill for display in early 1970 and is pictured there in the summer of 1973.
(Ron W. Cranham)

Pictured at Credenhill in 1983, the following year it was part of an exchange deal with W.B. of G.B., the R.A.F. Museum receiving a North American B-25J Mitchell for their collection. In return, W.B. of G.B. received TE392. It has remained in store for the last ten years.
(Alan M. Hewitt)

TE462

Spitfire L.F.XVIE TE462 was taken on charge by the R.A.F. in June 1945 and placed in store until 1950. She was issued to the Station Flight at Finningley in October the same year. In April 1951 TE462 suffered a flying accident and following repairs she was transferred to No. 101 F.R.S. This was to be her last flying unit as by the end of 1954 she was back in store. August 1955 saw her displayed at Ouston, remaining there until refurbished and presented to the Museum of Flight at East Fortune in Scotland in February 1971.

Spitfire L.F.XVIE TE462 began her Gate Guard duty at Ouston in 1955, seen there in August 1962, wearing the codes of No. 607 (County of Durham) R.Aux.A.F. *(Ron W. Cranham)*

Now minus markings, in 1966. By 1970 she was removed from Ouston and made ready for her new home - North of the Border at the Museum of Flight, East Fortune. *(M.A.P.)*

TE462 has been displayed at East Fortune since 1971. Seen here during 1989, she continues to be a popular exhibit. *(R. J. Major)*

TE476

Spitfire L.F.XVIE TE476 was taken on charge by the R.A.F. in June 1945 and placed in store until July 1951. She was then issued to No. 1 C.A.A.C.U. and flew with them until September 1956. After leaving this unit she ceased flying and became a display aircraft. She was selected in March 1958 to join the Station Flight at Biggin Hill, so she was brought back to flying condition again. This Flight was the forerunner to the Battle of Britain Flight. On a flight in September 1959 SL574, also with the Flight, suffered a forced landing on a cricket pitch in London. As a result of this, it was decided to ground TE476 as she was fitted with the same type of engine, and doubt was placed on its reliability. In January 1960 she was put on display at Neatishead, but during 1967 this Spitfire travelled to Henlow for use in the film "The Battle of Britain". Filming over, TE476 was refurbished, and then issued to Northolt for display, being removed in November 1988 as part of the R.A.F./H.F.L. exchange deal. This Spitfire is currently being restored to flying condition by Personal Plane Services at Booker airfield.

Spitfire L.F.XVIE TE476 at Coventry Airport in 1959, one of her last venues. Following the crash of SL574 on 20th September, 1959, TE476 being of the same type, age and also part of the then Historic Aircraft Flight, was subsequently grounded. *(M.A.P.)*

Settled into her role of Gate Guard, TE476 at Coltishall in May 1962, a station the new 'Battle of Britain Flight' operated from in 1963. *(Ron W. Cranham)*

From Coltishall TE476 moved to Neatishead, was then used in the film "The Battle of Britain", eventually arriving at Northolt for display in 1970. In 1988 she was removed being part of the R.A.F./H.F.L. exchange deal. *(Neil Randell)*

TE476 at Booker in 1994, her restoration to flying condition by Personal Plane Services is nearing completion. *(Richard H. Paver)*

PM651

Spitfire P.R.XIX PM651 was issued to the Civilian Repair Depot at White Waltham in November 1945. During September 1947 she was placed in store, remaining there until January 1951, when she was taken to Airwork General Trading and refurbished. With the work completed, PM651 returned to store, not emerging again until March 1954. She was issued to the THUM Flight at Woodvale later that month but suffered a flying accident in April. Following repair this Spitfire was put on display at Hucknall. From there she transferred to Andover, remaining on show until 1967, when she joined the other aeroplanes being assembled at Henlow for the film "The Battle of Britain". Following the film, PM651 was restored, then issued to the Exhibition Flight at Abingdon, remaining with them until 1973. Later that year she went on display at Benson and stayed until November 1989. She was then transferred to St. Athan for restoration prior to going on display at the R.A.F. Museum, but today PM651 is back in store at St. Athan.

PM651 pictured in September 1958 at Andover on Battle of Britain Day. The P.R.XIX version of the Spitfire was unarmed. In place of weapons, extra fuel tanks were fitted, giving it almost twice the fuel of the Fighter versions, thus allowing it to fly deep into enemy territory on reconnaissance missions. *(Richard S. Fell)*

PM651 in all silver finish with a red spinner at Andover in 1961. We can clearly see in this picture a camera port above the roundel and the doors for the retractable tail wheel. *(Ron W. Cranham)*

During 1967 PM651 left Benson and was used in the film "the Battle of Britain". Filming over, it went to Bicester for refurbishment. We see her there in 1972, once again painted in her P.R.U. scheme. *(Ron W. Cranham)*

PM651 returned to Benson for display in 1971, finally standing down in November 1989. *(Crown Copyright/M.O.D.)*

PS853

Spitfire P.R.XIX PS853 was taken on charge by the R.A.F. in January 1945. A few weeks later she joined No. 16 Squadron in Europe and flew with them until September, when she transferred to No. 268 Squadron (renumbered to No. 16 in October 1945). March 1946 saw PS853 return to the U.K. and be placed in store. In the early 1950's "853" was issued to the THUM Flight at Woodvale, and served with them until June 1957. She then ceased flying and moved to West Raynham for display during May 1958. PS853 was selected to join the Memorial Flight and so was brought up to flying condition in November 1962, eventually joining the Flight at Coltishall in April 1964. This aeroplane along with eleven other Spitfires, took part in the flying sequences for the film "The Battle of Britain", made during the late 1960's. When her film role was over, PS853 rejoined The Battle of Britain Memorial Flight and still serves with them.

In the 1950's PS853 joined the THUM Flight, she is seen here in this role at Woodvale in 1956. *(Chris J. Foulds/Ray C. Coulson)*

PS853 arrived at the Central Fighter Establishment, West Raynham for guard duty in 1959 but was not placed on the gate although she remained the Station mascot until the early 1960's when it was decided to return her to flying condition. *(Crown Copyright/M.O.D.)*

Benson in 1966, now a member of the renamed Battle of Britain Flight. *(Ron W. Cranham)*

PS853 at West Malling in 1989, finished in P.R.U. scheme and invasion stripes. She is one of five Spitfires operated by the BBMF. *(Neil Randell)*

PS915

Spitfire P.R.XIX PS915 was taken on charge by the R.A.F. in April 1945, joining No. 514 Squadron in June. By the end of the year PS915 had transferred to No. 11 Squadron, operating from bases in Germany. October 1946 saw her move again, going to No. 151 Repair and Service Unit at Luneburg. Her stay lasted until April 1947, when she returned to No. 11 Squadron. In July 1948 she was issued to No. 2 Communications Squadron, flying with them until her return to the U.K. in May 1951. PS915 was then placed in store until chosen to fly with the THUM Flight at Woodvale in June 1954. This was to be her final posting, serving the Flight until retired in June 1957. This Spitfire was then issued for display at West Malling. From there she passed to Leuchars, being displayed until 1967, when she joined other Spitfires at Henlow for use in the film "the Battle of Britain".

After filming, PS915 returned to Leuchars, staying until 1975. Next, this aeroplane moved to Brawdy in Wales, but in October 1977 she was used by the Battle of Britain Memorial Flight at Coningsby for engine installation test work, using a modified Rolls-Royce Griffon 58 engine from an Avro Shackleton. The successful outcome of these tests meant the Flight would now have a new source of engines for its MK XIX Spitfires. Following test work PS915 returned to Brawdy for display, remaining there until mid-1984.

It was then decided to restore PS915 to flying condition for the Battle of Britain Memorial Flight. She was transported to British Aerospace at Samlesbury, where the work was undertaken by staff and apprentices. She became airborne for the first time after her restoration on 20th November 1986. On 24th March 1987 this Spitfire was officially handed over to the Battle of Britain Memorial Flight at Coningsby, where she can currently be found.

Spitfire P.R.XIX PS915, while flying with No. 151 Repair and Servicing Unit from R.A.F. Luneburg in Germany during October 1946.
(Wally Rouse)

PS915 was to continue flying long after most U.K. Spitfires, when she joined the THUM Flight at Woodvale. She is seen looking quite tarnished against a snowy background at Speke Airport in February 1955. She was finally grounded in June 1957. *(Chris J. Foulds)*

PS915 at Leuchars, circa 1962, several features common to the P.R.XIX are evident in this picture. The curved windscreen in place of the standard bulletproof one, fitted for increased visibility. The intake below the exhaust stack was for the cabin blower, and to reduce problems with the pressurised cockpit, and the access door has been done away with. (A.P.N.)

Her last posting was to Brawdy, going on display in 1980. (M.A.P.)

PS915 is currently displayed in a scheme which represents one of the prototype Mk XIV's which were based round a modified MkVIII airframe. (Ron W. Cranham)

LA198

Spitfire F.21 LA198 was taken on charge by the R.A.F. during October 1944, going on to No. 1 Squadron in May 1945. She was placed in store in early October 1946, not being reissued until May 1947, when No. 602 (City of Glasgow) Squadron R.Aux.A.F. took her on charge. LA198 served with them until a flying accident required her to return to the manufacturers for repair. After the work had been carried out she was placed in store. It was September 1951 before this Spitfire joined her final flying unit, No. 3 C.A.A.C.U. November 1953 saw her return to the manufacturers. During February 1954, LA198, now relegated to display duties, was issued to No. 187 Squadron (A.T.C.) in Worcester. Like a lot of other Spitfires in 1967 this aeroplane travelled to Henlow for use in the film "The Battle of Britain". Following the film, she was restored and put on display at Locking in 1970. Her stay lasted nearly 16 years, then in the Spring of 1986, LA198 was transferred to Leuchars in Scotland, where she remained until 1989 when she was removed to St. Athan and is presently in store.

Spitfire F21 LA198 circa 1959 while displayed at No. 187 (A.T.C.) Squadron in Worcester. She finally left Worcester in 1967 to join the other aircraft assembled at Henlow for the film "The Battle of Britain". *(A.P.N.)*

April 1970 at Locking, we can see her in the markings first issued to her whilst with No. 1 Squadron in May 1945. She is complete with pilot in the cockpit! *(Crown Copyright/M.O.D.)*

During March 1986 LA198 was transferred to R.A.F. Leuchars in Scotland. We see her having the many coats of paint which had been applied over the years, removed prior to restoration. *(Crown Copyright/M.O.D.)*

LA198 on 6th June 1986 during her dedication service. Now in the codes issued whilst with No. 602 (City of Glasgow) Squadron R.Aux.A.F. *(John Bishop)*

LA226

Spitfire F.21 LA226 was taken on charge by the R.A.F. in February 1945, and joined No. 91 (Nigerian) Squadron the following month. She flew with them until returning to Vickers for modifications during July, then rejoined her Squadron. LA226 suffered a forced landing in August 1945 and after repair was transferred to No. 122 Squadron, arriving during January 1946. Her stay lasted until December 1947, when LA226 was placed in store. She was issued to her last unit, No. 3 C.A.A.C.U. in September 1951, operating with them until January 1954. Shortly afterwards this Spitfire could be seen on display with No. 2224 (A.T.C.) Squadron at Albrighton. At some later date she was stored at Cosford, then transferred to Little Rissington in 1958. Like so many Spitfires, LA226 moved to Henlow in 1967 for the film "the Battle of Britain". Although not used herself, she did provide parts for other aeroplanes which were. After the film this Spitfire was restored and displayed at the South Marston factory, where she was built by Vickers in 1945, leaving in 1984 to join SL674 at Biggin Hill. In 1988 this Spitfire was stored at Shawbury, then in September 1992 LA226 transferred to St. Athan and is currently one of eight Spitfires held at this station.

This well-thumbed picture dating back to 1956, shows a young Bob Griffiths on the wing of LA226 while it was stored at Cosford. Many years later Bob became Flt. Lt. R. Griffiths R.A.F.V.R. Commanding Officer of No. 196 (Walsall) Squadron A.T.C. *(Robert Griffiths)*

LA226 still at Cosford circa 1957, the code letter "E" was issued while flying with No. 3 C.A.A.C.U. at Exeter in September 1951.
(M.A.P.)

This Spitfire first went on display at Little Rissington in the late 1950's. Seen here in 1965 painted in the markings issued to her whilst flying with No. 91 Squadron towards the end of W.W.II.
(Ron W. Cranham)

During 1970 LA226 went on display at Vickers South Marston plant, the factory where she was built in 1945.
(Paul Charles)

LA226 seen in corrosion inhibiting zinc oxide primer during 1988 at Shawbury.
(Crown Copyright/ M.O.D./ Patricia Shelley)

LA255

Spitfire F21 LA255 was taken on charge by the R.A.F. in April 1945, being issued to No. 1 Squadron in June the same year. She is said to have been with No. 91 Squadron briefly, before returning to her manufacturers for modifications during July. Early in 1946 LA255 was returned to No. 1 Squadron but her flying days came to an end after a flying accident in November 1947. Following repairs she was issued to Tangmere as an instructional airframe. During the 1950's this Spitfire was displayed at Cardington and remained there until the early 1960's. LA255 once again joined No. 1 Squadron at their West Raynham base, moving with them to Wittering, where she is, very wisely, displayed in the summer months and kept in a hangar for the rest of the year.

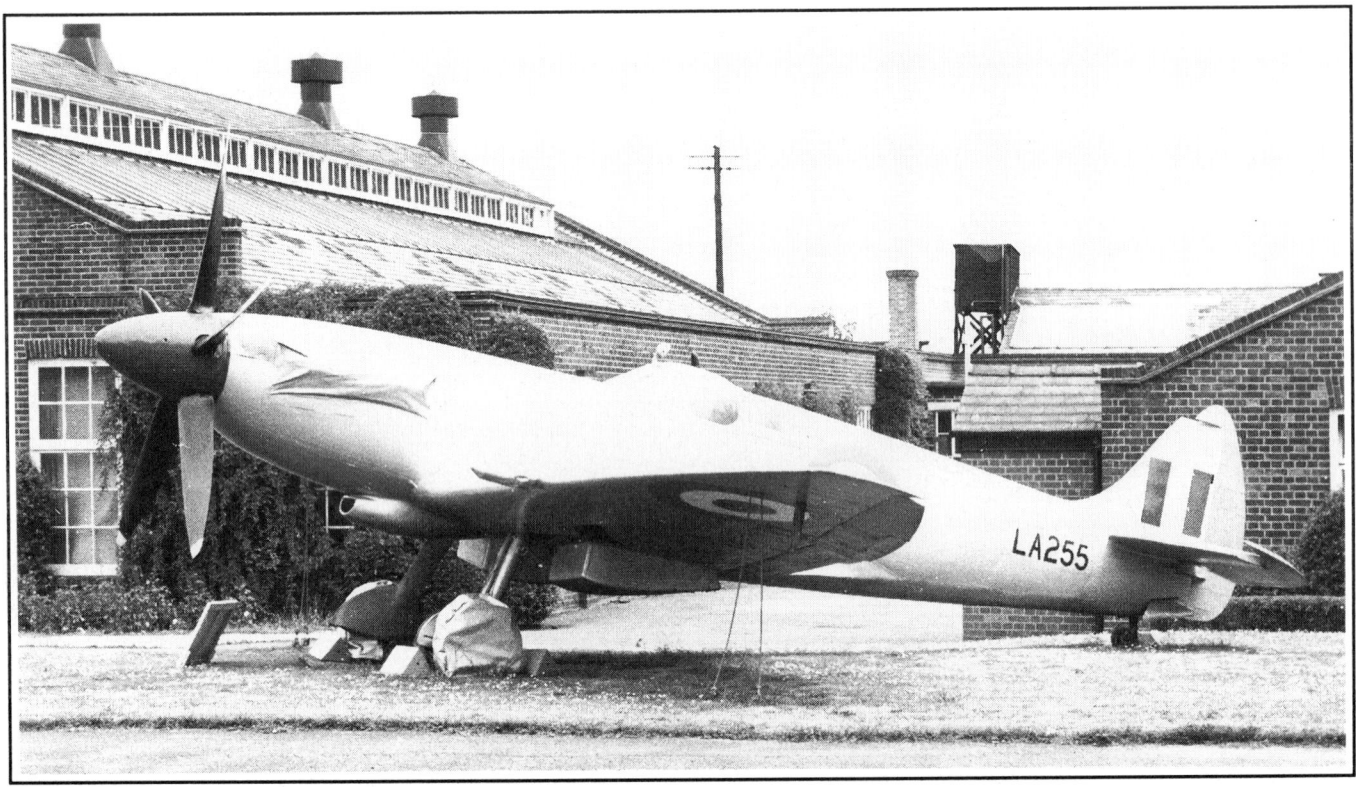

Spitfire F.21 LA255 whilst displayed at Cardington circa 1957.   *(M.A.P.)*

LA255 was reunited with her former Squadron (No. 1) at West Raynham in October 1966. Note the Hawker Hunter of No. 1 Squadron in the background.
(Ron W. Cranham)

When No. 1 Squadron moved to Wittering, LA255 moved with them. She is painted in the markings she wore whilst flying with No. 1 Squadron in the late 1940's. *(Alan Hewitt)*

When all Spitfire Gate Guard were removed from display, following M.O.D. policy, LA255 was exempt, having such strong Squadron ties. *(Crown Copyright/M.O.D.)*

PK624

Spitfire F.22 PK624 was taken on charge by the R.A.F. in December 1945, and placed in store until returning to her manufacturers for modifications during December 1946. Following the work she was once again placed in store. Eventually, in August 1948 PK624 was issued to No. 614 (County of Glamorgan) Squadron R.Aux.A.F., serving with this unit until being transferred to A.G.T. at Gatwick for refurbishment in January 1951.

PK624 saw little use over the following years and, by 1958, could be seen on display at Uxbridge. Her next move came in 1963, travelling to Northolt where she remained until the late 1960's. This Spitfire was restored before moving to Abingdon in 1970, and since 1989 she has been stored at St. Athan.

PK624 in April 1958 displayed at Uxbridge. For some reason she has been given the serial of a de Havilland Chipmunk, WP916.
(A. Pearcy/Chris J. Foulds)

During 1963 PK624 moved to Northolt for display. We can see she has been repainted, and her correct serial re-applied.
(M.A.P.)

PK624 was moved to Abingdon in 1970. We see her during 1987 wearing the markings of a No. 614 (County of Glamorgan) Squadron R.Aux.A.F. aircraft, a unit she flew with in the late 1940's.
(Neil Randell)

Now at St. Athan, following removal from gate duty during 1989. We can see in this shot that on the Mk22 (and Mk24) the tail has grown again, to counter the power of the Rolls Royce Griffon 61 engine. In the hangar behind is a Mosquito TT35.
(Ray C. Coulson)

PK664

Spitfire F.22 PK664 was taken on charge by the R.A.F. in December 1945 and placed in store until March 1947. She then returned to the manufacturers for modifications. PK664 was stored again until she was finally issued to No.615 (County of Surrey) Squadron in May 1949. This was to be her only flying unit, serving with them until December 1950. Once again PK664 was placed in store. In February 1954 she was sold back to Vickers but the demand for Spitfires had dwindled, so she was eventually put on display at Waterbeach, later passing on to West Raynham. Her final posting came in 1962 with a move to Binbrook, remaining there until the station closed in 1989, and has since then been stored at St. Athan.

Spitfire F.22 PK664 in all silver finish at Waterbeach in March 1961. Of the 260 Mark F.22's built, PK664 is one of only four that have survived. *(Ron W. Cranham)*

By 1962 PK664 had moved to Binbrook and is wearing fictitious Squadron codes. *(Ron W. Cranham)*

During the 1960's she was restored in the markings worn whilst flying with No .615 (County of Surrey) Squadron but by June 1969 she was looking quite shabby. Even one of her cannons is sagging. *(Ron W. Cranham)*

1987 and still at Binbrook, PK664 looking more like her former self, now pylon-mounted and displayed at the Station gate. With the closure of the Station she was placed in store at St. Athan. *(M.A.P.)*

PK683

Spitfire F. 24 PK683 was taken on charge by the R.A.F. in August 1946, and placed in store until 1950. She was then selected for service in the Far East, arriving in Singapore during September that year. The information given on her movement card tells of a flying accident in July 1951. Following repairs, PK683 joined the Singapore Auxiliary Air Force. February 1952 saw her damaged again and issued to No. 390 Maintenance Unit for repairs. She was not reissued for operational flying, and was struck off charge in April 1954. This Spitfire originally went to the Malayan Air Training Corps for display, later moving to Changi. In June 1970 she returned to Great Britain and was placed in store at Bicester, transferring to Kemble in June 1972. In November PK683 was issued to Colerne for display. This Spitfire was placed on permanent exhibition at the R. J. Mitchell Hall of Aviation in Southampton in February 1976.

PK683 in pleasant surroundings at Fairy Point in Singapore in June 1961. *(Peter R. Arnold Collection)*

During the 1960's PK683 was transferred to the Headquarters of the Far East Air Force at Changi. Seen here wearing a very dubious colour scheme. *(Peter R. Arnold Collection)*

PK683 looking factory fresh in June 1975 whilst displayed at Colerne. *(Ron W. Cranham)*

February 1976 saw PK683 travel to her final home, the R. J. Mitchell Hall of Aviation in Southampton. *(Spitfire Society/David Green)*

Spitfire F. 24 PK724 was taken on charge by the R.A.F. in October 1946 and placed in store until April 1949. She then travelled to Westland Aircraft for modifications and was ready for collection by February 1950. Following the work, PK724 went back into store. Declared a non-effective airframe in December 1954, this Spitfire moved to Norton for display in November 1955. She went on to be displayed at Gaydon in 1961, but during 1967 was moved to Henlow for use in the film "The Battle of Britain". Due to technical problems she was not used and was returned to Gaydon. With the closure of this Station, PK724 moved to Finningley in 1970, and was restored prior to being displayed at the R.A.F. Museum in 1971.

Spitfire F. 24 PK724 seen in all silver finish while at Norton in 1957. This Spitfire is said to have flown a total of only seven hours.
(G. Bowtle/Peter R. Arnold Collection)

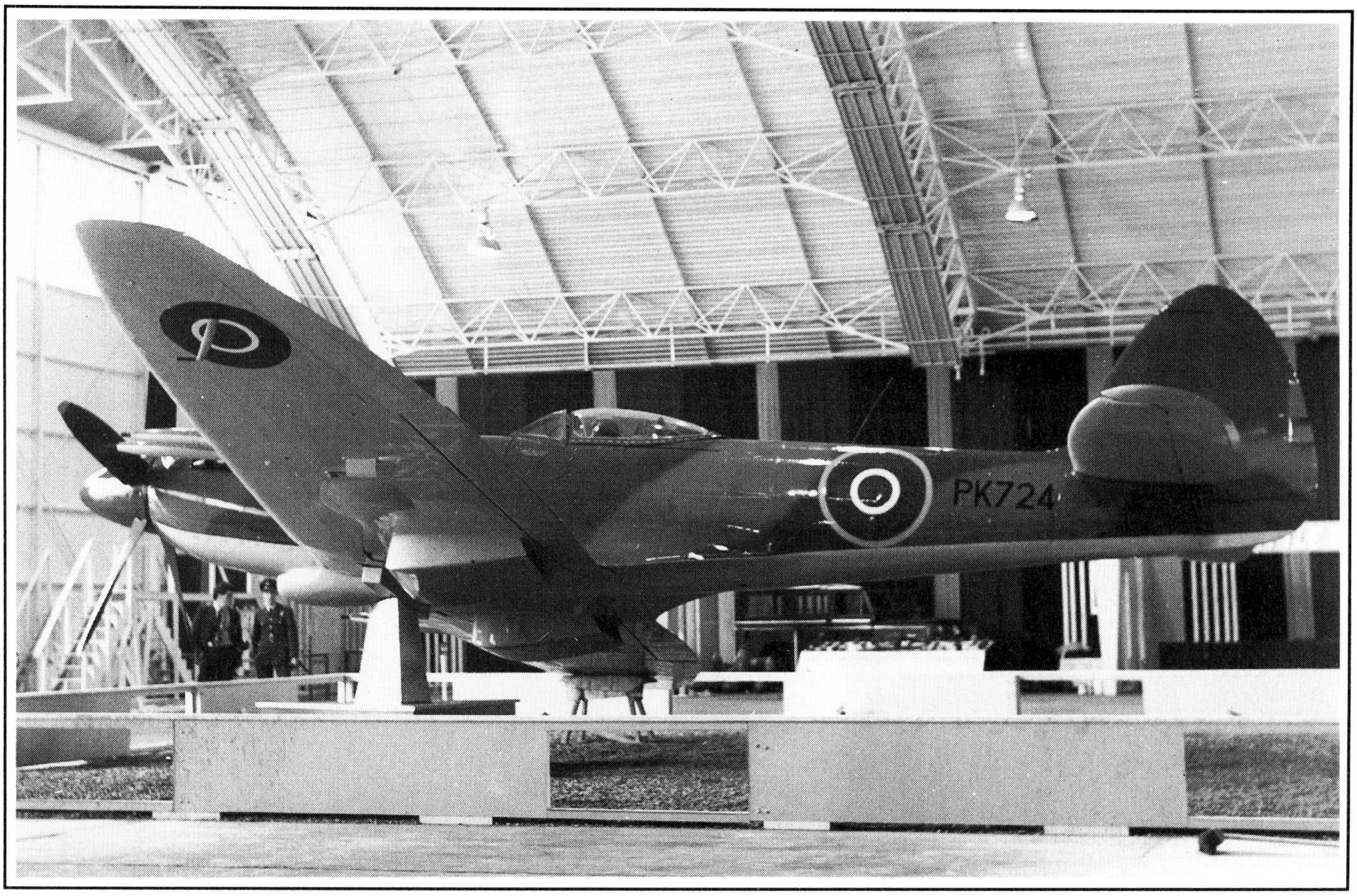

PK724 at Gaydon in September 1969. Notice the flush fitting undercarriage doors as fitted to the later Marks of Spitfire. An increase in streamlining meant an all important increase in speed. *(Ron W. Cranham)*

With the closure of Gaydon, PK724 was made ready for display at the R.A.F. Museum, Hendon and arrived there in 1971. *(Chris Shelton)*

VN485

Spitfire F. 24 VN485 was taken on charge by the R.A.F. in September 1947, and placed in store until June 1949. She was selected for service with the R.A.F. in the Far East, arriving at Seletar in August the same year. She was placed in store before being issued to No. 80 Squadron in October 1950. An accident at the end of the year required major repairs. VN485 was returned to her unit, serving with them until April 1955. Her final flight took place during that month when, in the company of three other Spitfires, another F24 and two Mark P.R.XIX's, they carried out a fly-past at Kai Tak air base on the occasion of the Queen's birthday. VN485 was then grounded and began her role of display aircraft in September 1956, at R.A.F. Kai Tak with the Royal Hong Kong Auxiliary Air Force. This Spitfire finally returned home in July 1989 and was placed on display at the Imperial War Museum, Duxford.

VN485 seen at Kai Tak in the 1960's, one feature of the natural finish or silver painted aeroplane was the black anti-glare panel applied to the area in front of the cockpit to prevent the pilot being dazzled by the sun. *(N. A. MacDougall)*

Still in the 1960's, dummy cannons have now been fitted, the F. 24 was equipped with two 20mm. British Hispano Mark V cannons per wing. The two inner cannons had 175 rounds per gun, the outer had 150 rounds per gun. *(Ron W. Cranham)*

VN485 returned to the U.K. in July 1989 and is displayed by the Imperial War Museum at Duxford. Although usually kept in a hangar, on a fine day she is often seen outside. *(Chris Shelton)*

Spitfires on the Big Screen

There were two particular occasions during which the Spitfires depicted in this book were used in films. Firstly in 1955 came "Reach for the Sky", the story of Fighter Ace Douglas Bader, filmed at Kenley. The other was "The Battle of Britain" made in 1968. Below are two lists based on information supplied by Spitfire Historian Peter R. Arnold, detailing the aeroplanes used and the role they played in these films.

Reach for the Sky

RR263 L.F.XVIE This Spitfire was issued to Kenley for display duty at the time the film was being made. It has been suggested that she took part as airfield dressing, but as yet there is no photographic proof to support this claim.

SL574 L.F.XVIE This aeroplane with three other Spitfires took part in the flying sequences of the film.

TE288 L.F.XVIE This aeroplane was used for airfield dressing and was thought to have been used for close-up shots taken in the studio.

TE311 L.F.XVIE Although made available for use in the film, she was not in fact ferried to Kenley.

TB752 L.F.XVIE As above.

The Battle of Britain

BL614	F.VB	This aeroplane was restored to taxiing condition.
EP120	L.F.VB	Used for Airfield dressing.
MK356	L.F.IXC	Used for Airfield dressing.
RW382	L.F.XVIE	Used for Airfield dressing.
SL574	L.F.XVIE	Used for Airfield dressing.
SM411	L.F.XVIE	Restored to taxiing condition.
TB382	L.F.XVIE	Restored to taxiing condition.
TE311	L.F.XVIE	Restored to taxiing condition.
TE356	L.F.XVIE	Restored to taxiing condition.
TE384	L.F.XVIE	Restored to taxiing condition.
TE476	L.F.XVIE	Restored to taxiing condition.
PM651	P.R.XIX	Used for Airfield dressing.
PS853	P.R.XIX	One of the 12 Spitfires used in the flying sequences of the film.
PS915	P.R.XIX	Used for Airfield dressing.
LA198	F.21	Used for Airfield dressing.

The following four Spitfires were delivered to Henlow but did not appear in the film.

BM597 F.VB As an early Mk Spitfire BM597 was not used in the film but dispatched to Pinewood Studios and used to make the moulds from which the replica Spitfires were produced.

TE184 L.F.XVIE Due to her poor condition she was not used but dispatched to Finningley for restoration.

LA226 F.21 This Spitfire donated parts to other Spitfires used in the film.

PK724 F.24 Whilst at Henlow her engine was started up with very little trouble, however, her wiring harness was burnt out during the installation of a radio, subsequently PK724 was returned to Gaydon.

Restoration

The most positive act to stem from the removal of Spitfire Gate Guards from display, many of which are now in private hands, has been the desire to see them flying again. Currently (as of August 1994) eight are airworthy, and a further nine are in varying states of restoration. There two groups can be found in the following lists.

Airworthy

MK732	L.F.IXC	R. Neth.A.F. Deelen or Rijen Air Bases, Netherlands.
RW382	L.F.XVIE	H.F.L., Audley End, Saffron Walden, Essex, U.K.
TD248	L.F.XVIE	Earls Colne, Essex, U.K.
TE184	L.F.XVIE	Myrick Aviation, Jersey, Channel Isles.
TE356	L.F.XVIE	Pinal Air Park, Marana, Arizona, U.S.A.
TE384	L.F.XVIE	Toowoomba, Queensland, Australia.
PS853	P.R.XIX	B.B.M.F., R.A.F. Coningsby, Lincs., U.K.
PS915	P.R.XIX	B.B.M.F., R.A.F. Coningsby, Lincs., U.K.

Under Restoration

AR614	F.VC	Acquired by Sir Tim Wallis for the Alpine Fighter Collection in New Zealand and is being restored by H.F.L., Audley End, Saffron Walden, Essex, U.K.
BM597	F.VB	H.F.L., Audley End, Saffron Walden, Essex, U.K.
EP120	L.F.VB	Owned by The Fighter Collection and is being restored by H.F.L. at Audley End.
MK356	L.F.IXC	R.A.F. St. Athan, Glamorgan, Wales.
RW386	L.F.XVIE	Florida, U.S.A. (Stored dismantled, awaiting a decision on her fate).
SL542	L.F.XVIE	Lakeland, Florida, U.S.A.
TB252	L.F.XVIE	H.F.L. Audley End, Saffron Walden, Essex, U.K.
TD135	L.F.XVIE	Genesio State, New York, U.S.A.
TE476	L.F.XVIE	Personal Plane Services, Booker, Bucks., U.K.